Hope!

Deborah Blaney Ward.

Silently
Weeping

DEBORAH BLANEY WARD

Produced by:

FriesenPress
Suite 300 – 852 Fort Street
Victoria, BC, Canada V8W 1H8

www.friesenpress.com

Distributed to the trade by The Ingram Book Company

Table of Contents

DEDICATIONS

This book is dedicated to my children, who travelled with me on part of this journey. I hope that this will give you some understanding as to who I am.

I love you all so very much.

Deborah Blaney Ward

ACKNOWLEDGEMENTS

To Earl, for your continued support and love during this writing process. You wiped my tears as I relived these memories and listened when I needed to speak. You supported me in this long process and never complained (well almost never) when I was deep in thought and zoned out from conversations around me.

To my brother Eric, thank you for agreeing to be part of this book and for your support in all that we went through and standing behind me. Hopefully acknowledgement will set us free.

To my sister Susanne, for your endless support through the years and for helping me fill in the blanks. Your selfless belief in me and all that I went through has helped me so much and your encouragement to keep going on this project boosted my belief in myself.

To Nino, for reading every page, for correcting my mistakes and for your comments of encouragement that helped me put this all together. I can't thank you enough. I sincerely appreciate all your help.

To my dear friend Crystal (Cris), without your friendship I would be lost. You have been here for me for over 20 years. We have laughed together, cried together, did so many things together and prayed together. We are so much alike. Our friendship holds no bounds.

To Maureen who took the time to read my manuscript and who offered her opinions and comments. I hope you are happy with the results.

I have so much love for all of you.

I hope that this book gives encouragement to whoever reads it. There is hope, there is always hope. Believe in yourself and never give up.

INSPIRATIONS

Deborah I am so proud to say that I am your sister. I congratulate you on being able to put your story on paper, as I know you had to relive each and every moment of your journey in this life over again. Where you are today in your personal being is a miracle that you are to be commended for. Your strength, courage and belief in God have been an inspiration and hope for me as I am sure it will be for all who read your story.

Your loving sister, Susanne

PROLOGUE

PAIN – Everyone at some point experiences pain of some kind. The dictionary describes pain as a physical or mental suffering; hurting; trouble; exertion; to cause distress to.

I have experienced pain in almost every way imaginable. The pain of injury, the pain of child abuse, the pain of rape, the pain of failed marriages, the pain of mental abuse and the pain of death of a loved one. This is the never ending pain of a life lived and living life. I have survived all of this and I sometimes wonder how I did it.

Memories can be a wonderful thing, they can also be very painful and until you come face to face with your demons you can't move on in your life. This was a lesson I was going to learn the hard way because I could not accept the one thing that happened to me and so my life was set in a spinning motion that was going to take a very long time to stop. The events in my life were not of my own doing and it took a long time for me to realize that. The guilt that I carried for years over matters that I had absolutely no control over, took control of me. I was its prisoner for almost 40 years. Then things started to slowly change. I changed and this is the story of me.

Many people who knew about my life suggested I should write a book. My first reaction was to laugh, saying, "Why? No one would believe it."

The only person, who knows what it was like, is me. But where would I start? So much has happened. Where would I begin? Well, I thought, maybe I should start at the beginning.

THE BEGINNING

My mother was born in 1924 and raised in Greenock, Scotland in an area close to the docks where the ships would come in. They were poor. She was the youngest of 11 children. My mother didn't have to learn to cook and clean, the older kids did all the work. Her father died when she was about 10 years old and her mother was left to look after all the kids. Mom was about 5'4, brunette, a slim figure and quite attractive. From what I can understand, some of the older kids were working part time to help out their mother. Apparently she ran the home with an iron fist in order to keep everyone in line. My mother never talked too much about her young life other than having to learn how to play the piano, which she didn't want to do. She talked about her siblings and seemed to be close to one brother, Bill. The only information I really remember from her was that one sister, Ria, seemed to have made good in her life. She was very fashionable and liked and accumulated a lot of expensive jewellery. She married a man the family was not happy about and a couple of years after the marriage she died mysteriously. She had a brother Patrick who died of tuberculosis at home. My mother was exposed to this and it would show up later in her life. Her sister Alice was an artist. She drew for her own pleasure but was talented enough to be offered work as a commercial artist. She refused, explaining that her art was strictly for her personal satisfaction. I have a book of some of her drawings and poetry that she did. My mother and Alice would write to each other in rhyme, telling of what was happening to them and friends around them. The book has just a few drawings but the talent displayed is quite obvious.

Mom worked in a torpedo factory during the war and would tell us stories about the bombings that happened over Scotland. It was a very scary time for all during the Second World War and she would tell us about running to bomb shelters. One night in particular, the Germans were flying directly overhead and they had no idea what to expect. She said they held their breath until they left the area. They had to hide inside the building and no one made a sound. When it was over they realized how close they came to being caught. The factory was the safest place to work because if the German's captured the town, they would want the factory and the laboratory that was next door to it.

As I said earlier all the siblings would give up a portion of their pay checks to help out their mother and when my mother became ill with dementia in her final years she would tell us she had to go get her pay check to give to her mother.

Mom would talk about the dances she would go to during the war. Sailors would come there looking for a little female companionship and a few drinks. Mom often said this was one of her best times in her life and she had a ball. Her and her friend Margaret would save their money for the weekend of fun and meeting different guys. They would go to the movie houses and the dances but the dances were their favourite spot. She would tell us of all the guys they met and the fun they would have. Mom also informed us that at this time she was engaged to a man named "Ronnie". That was all we knew of him. She had one picture of him that she kept and she told us how he was horribly upset when she broke the engagement. Apparently his sister begged her to reconsider but she didn't. I think this was a decision that she came to regret quite quickly soon after. Her reason for the indecision? She met my father.

My father was born in Milltown, (St. Stephen) New Brunswick in 1924 but was raised in Windsor, Ontario. His father, my grandfather was the son of immigrants who settled in the New Brunswick area on a grant of land given to Irish settlers. This was farming land and sons were to carry it on. My grandfather was not interested in farming and joined the military. During World War One, my grandfather served over seas in England and met my grandmother. They married and he brought her back to Milltown. After the war my grandfather got his teacher's degree and taught school for a while but times were hard. My grandparents had purchased a home in Milltown. He improved the property by adding a barn. He was broke, rented the home out to a relative and he uprooted the family and went to Windsor, Ontario. He found work with the Ford Motor Company and life improved. They had 5 children. My father was 5'8", slim build, and dark brown hair and dark brown eyes. He would be considered a handsome man. He was raised believing that he was God's gift to women as he was idealized by his mother and his sisters. He was quite the Casanova.

My father graduated from Hon. W.D. Kennedy Collegiate Institute and then enrolled at W.D. Lowe Technical School where he studied electronics. He read everything he could find on the subject and it became his hobby. He eventually had his own radio and TV repair shop. When the Second World War began, he signed up from Lowe Tech. He lied about his age and joined the Navy. His ship was sent to Greenock, Scotland and there he met my mother in 1945.

They met at a dance hall and my father pursued my mother. In November 1945 my father married my mother and brought her home to Canada as a war bride in 1946. That was the first mistake. They should never have married. My mother was pregnant with my sister (she was not pregnant before the wedding) during her journey across the ocean. Because of the pregnancy she had to cross on a medical ship, the Lady Nelson, along with other wives in the same condition. My father was aware of the pregnancy but I am unsure if my grandparents knew of it. My grandparents', especially my grandmother did not approve of this marriage. So, upon arrival in Canada they immediately set out to destroy the marriage. She wanted my father to put my mother back on the boat and get the marriage annulled. That was impossible because she was pregnant and a Catholic. Divorce was absolutely out of the question. So she began to live out the reality of her life with him and his mother. It was going to be hell. The reason for the hostility was that Dad was engaged to my grandmother's best friend's daughter before leaving to serve in the war. There was to be a grand wedding when he returned and all would be well. They would have the house and the white picket fence and all the world would be in harmony. But then the telegram arrived to announce that he had fallen in love and married a Scottish gal and he was bringing her home. All hell was about to break loose.

My father arrived in Ontario before my mother. He was to set up a residence and make things ready for my mother when she arrived. When he arrived home his mother, the ex-fiancée and the ex-fiancée's mother had a party arranged at my grand-parent's house. During the party Dad and the ex disappeared for a while. The whole scheme was to make him want the ex and send my mother packing even before she boarded the boat. He should have admitted that he made a mistake and leave her with her family but he was a selfish and controlling man and he made the arrangements to bring her over.

When my mother arrived, pregnant, the tongues started wagging. My grandmother counted out the time frame of the pregnancy to see if my father had been "trapped", but time would prove she had not trapped him. My parents were married in November and my sister Susanne was born at the end of September. Mom struggled with a language barrier due to the heavy Scottish brogue and, of course, the different meanings for different words in the English language. Apparently simple sayings like "I'll ring you up some time," meaning "I'll phone you" would set people up to fits of laughter and, of course there was the, "I'll knock you up sometime soon," meaning " I'll knock on your door".All this would send my grandmother's blood pressure sky high, "it was a disgrace that this woman could not speak proper English." So my mother was in this marriage with a man whom she apparently loved and was willing to do anything for and he was in the marriage to have a front, of the good Canadian Navy man who looks after the home fires with a woman who didn't have a clue about keeping house and home. It was almost immediately after my mother arrived in Canada that he started running around on her. And so this was the life that we were to have unfolded before our very eyes on a daily basis.As little children we watched and heard the verbal abuse of his name calling and ridicule. She wanted to have him want and love her, but it was rare occasions when he showed any feelings. I believe he enjoyed demoralizing her. Interestingly, he never left her. The cat always came home for the cream. He knew she loved him and would do anything to try and please him. Loving him was her biggest downfall and I feel caused her to be unstable.

MILITARY LIFE

Life in the military always includes the possibility of being transferred to another Naval base. Their first transfer was to Halifax, N.S. While in Halifax my mother gave birth to a second sibling. Shortly thereafter my Dad left the navy for a couple of years and returned to Windsor, Ont. He then re-enlisted and their next transfer was to Sorel, Quebec. This is where I was born on April 11, 1954, Easter Sunday. It was a French hospital where very few people spoke English. Apparently my mother was trying to tell the nurse that the baby was coming but the nurse had no clue as to what she was talking about. I guess my mother had just made it to the bed and the nurse checked her and went running. I was more than on the way. Shortly after my birth, we were transferred back to Halifax. We lived in the Military housing area known as Shannon Park. Our apartment was number six on the top floor – 8J. Since there were no elevators we had to walk up all six flights of stairs.

My sister Susanne tells me that I had boils as an infant and that I cried a lot. Dad would leave the house if he was in town and leave my mother alone with three kids, an eight year old, a six year old and me, newborn. I found out later in life that there was a child before me. They had a son that was still born. This was due to a thrashing my mother took from my father while he was drunk. They were fighting about his drinking and womanizing. The fight became physical. He struck her a severe blow to the stomach causing her to start in labour. It was in

January and the ambulance attendants strapped her in with a warm wool blanket over her. She told them that the baby was coming and they told her they would be at the hospital soon. The baby boy suffocated. She never did anything about it. Life for her seemed to be a constant nightmare.

I was around two or three years old when I became conscious of the tension and fighting between Mom and Dad. I remember my siblings crying and begging them to stop fighting. But they wouldn't and things would be thrown across the room and then Dad would leave and be gone for the night. Mom in her fury would take her temper out on us. Sometimes she would lock herself in the bathroom and threaten that she was going to commit suicide. Sometimes she would just strike out at us. Eventually he would come home and it would be good for a bit and then it would start all over again.

Dad had a side business of fixing radios and televisions. I believe that this was his way of meeting more women and there were lots of them. He would leave us for months at a time, sailing with the Navy and sometimes living with another woman when he was home. Mom would have to fend for us the best way she could. She would call the Military office to get him to give her some money. That would work once or twice and then we would be back to`` bumming" from neighbours. I hated it when Mom would send us to borrow something from the neighbours. It made you feel embarrassed and humiliated and the neighbours were getting tired of it. Sometimes they wouldn't answer the door even though you could hear their television. Other times I could hear comments about the "damn" Blaneys bumming again. I would hang my head in shame and move on.

Dad would be away a lot with his military duties and would bring us back gifts from the different places he visited. These were the good times. When the ship docked Mom would dress us up and we would go to meet the ship. It was a lot of fun and very exciting. We'd go home and Dad would give us the presents. Mom and Dad were affectionate with each other and eventually we would be told to go and play. These were bright beautiful moments but very quickly the darkness would return.

We had some beautiful pieces of china that he brought home. We didn't have them long. He of course would go and meet up with his latest flavour and the next thing you knew he was wearing that new piece of china. We had a China Doll, a statue that was the most beautiful thing I had ever seen. It was on the coffee table in the living room and I would look at it every day. One night he came home from a rendezvous and a fight broke out. We kids woke up to the screaming and hollering and then the throwing would start. Mom picked up the statue and threw it at him. I don't know if she hit him or not, but my beautiful China Doll was shattered into a million pieces. He left again and we kids were left to clean up the mess. At a very young age I began to pray that he wouldn't come home. But he always did.

There was hardly any money for food or clothes. We sometimes got hand- me- downs from whatever girlfriend he had at the time. Most times we got from one particular family. Dad had one drinking buddy who had a wife and family. The wife was just as heavy a drinker as they were and they would party together a lot. Their kids were about the same age as my sisters and they would get the hand me downs from them. They were so out of style when we got them that we were embarrassed to wear them but they were clothes and we didn't have any say about it. It was, "wear them or wear nothing".However, we did have one good outfit, our Sunday clothes.

My mother, having been raised a good Roman Catholic, made us go to church with her every Sunday and then go to Sunday school. We had to put on a good front for the people that all was well in the house. We weren't fooling anyone. They all knew and after a while, the pretense was dropped and it was just us kids who were made to go to Church. Dad never went.

He always told us he was no micky but when he married Mom he agreed to allow her to raise us in the Catholic faith and so off to Church we would go.

I remember one fight in particular. It was the usual. He had probably been drinking with his new woman. Mom was waiting for him when he came home. The hollering and screaming woke us up and we went to the living room. Mom was holding a knife and told him to get out. Dad was sitting there taunting her, and saying terrible things to us about her. We begged him to leave but he got up and made a grab for the knife, she pulled back and his hand was slit open. Instead of leaving and getting medical help he sat there and made us look at the blood pouring out of his hand saying things like, "Look at that? Look at what your mother did to me! Isn't this nice"? He grabbed a dish cloth and wrapped his hand in it and left. We kids cleaned up the mess. I think that was the first time that I realized that my mother was unstable. She could not leave him because she loved him and there was no one she could turn to. Back then you made your bed and you lay in it. Divorce was not a word that was discussed. You married for life, good or bad.

So in the first seven years of my life, I learned three important lessons. First, my father was not like other Dads who were devoted to their families. Second, my mother would not let go of him no matter what. And third we were her punching bags.

While he was at sea, a monthly bursary was sent home to the wives. The navy did not state how much to send home, it was up to the individual. Most of the time it was not enough money. He had to have his smokes and his totties as well as money for the port calls. Mom would send one of us to the post office to pick up the checks. By the time she cashed it and paid the people she owed, there was practically nothing left and we would start the process all over again. Mom was a smoker and she was miserable if she didn't have her smokes. I remember one time when she sent me to the store for cigarettes and my friend and I had played along the way. By the time we got to the store, I forgot what I had been sent for and my friend and I bought candy with the money. When I got home without the cigarettes, Mom gave me a beating that no young child should have to endure. I was sore for a week and she wouldn't let me forget it. I think I was 5 years old and she treated me like she hated me. My siblings went through the same thing with Mom. She would strike out at us for any reason. If she wanted to go to one of the neighbours (each building held seven apartments) and one of the older girls weren't home to watch me she would have a fit. Visiting with the neighbours was my mother's only source of adult conversations. She would scream and holler at my sisters, drag them in by the hair and then go out as if nothing happened. Mom was the neighbourhood bum, always borrowing something from anyone. When my siblings got older, if they had boyfriends, she would ask them for stuff. It was very embarrassing for them. I remember one time when Dad was home, he had built himself a small travel trailer. It was actually quite nice and he had it parked in the extra parking area in the park. Unfortunately for me, again I was 5 or 6, my father had bill collectors after him and one had come to the house looking for him. Somehow he had found out that Dad had this trailer and it was an asset and they wanted the information on it from Mom. Mom played stupid, telling the guy over and over that she didn't know anything about it and then I walked in. I told the guy everything he wanted to know. What it looked like, where it was parked. Everything. The guy left with all the info he needed. My mother immediately began beating me with all the fury of a person completely out of control. My mouth was so swollen from the punching and my ribs and legs were black and blue from the kicking. She had beaten me so bad I couldn't even talk. Then she locked me in my room to wait for my father to come home. I was so stunned from the beating; I don't know how long I was in the room. I remember my father coming in the room and looking at me. He never offered any comfort to me and left me still on the bed sobbing to myself. All he said was, "I guess your mother took care of it." Neither parent sought medical attention for me. There were no child abuse laws back then and they could do as they pleased. The next day I was expected to get up and go to school like nothing happened. This time, the school nurse was in the school and saw me. She called home and had my mother pick me up and suggested I get checked for broken ribs. That never happened. They just kept me home for a week.

I was terrified of my mother as you never knew when or why she would blow up. I feared my father. My father never ever laid a hand on me but the looks and tone of voice were enough to make me cringe. You could never do anything right for him. Dad was a mental abuser; Mom was a mental and physical abuser. If you mouthed back at her, you got a punch in the mouth. If you were late getting home, she would wait behind the door and would grab you by the hair and pull you in. Then there was the "knuckle". She would curl up her middle finger and would hit you in the head with it or in the chest. It hurt tremendously and she would do it over and over until you begged her to stop. Most times she would have you by the hair with one hand and the knuckle going with the other so you had no chance to avoid the blows. Struggling would end up with you losing a lot of hair and being covered with bruises. Sometimes these beatings resulted in a bloody nose and she would mockingly ask you, what you did that for? If you answered her and said that she did it, she would deny it. I remember one time when I sauced her, I said under my breath, "Shut up", as she was screaming at me for something. She heard me and ran after me. I locked myself in the bathroom and stayed there for a couple of hours. She started talking to me outside the door telling me it was OK to come out, that she was over it. At first I said "no" and then she started breaking me down. I knew I couldn't stay there forever and finally she told me to get out of there as she needed to use the bathroom and I opened the door. She was waiting for me. With all the force she could muster she slapped me in the mouth. As I recoiled and staggered she continued slapping me over and over. She told me she would knock every tooth out of my mouth if I ever spoke back to her again. I never did. I was learning by the age of 6 to stay out of her way as much as possible. Living in a very small 3 bedroom apartment, it wasn't easy.

Mom instilled other fears in us. She was frightened by thunder and lightning storms. She hated them. If a storm started during the night she would wake us up and herd us into a closet. The closet was central in the apartment and there were no windows in the area. She would make us sit in there with her and every time there was a clap of thunder or lightning she would begin praying out loud and almost paralyze us with her fear. When the storm became quiet she would have one of us check to see if it was over. We would pray it was done. If there was so much as a rumble, we would be in there for another hour. We learned from her to be afraid of it.

She also had a fear of water. When she was little she almost drowned and therefore would not have anything to do with going into the water. When we would go to the beach, she would have a fit because she was afraid something would happen and made it unpleasant for us. Dad would always tell her to be quiet. Typically, they would stop talking, then argue, then fight .Through it all, we had to play like everything was all right. Somehow, we all ended up learning to swim and my siblings got into canoeing and boating. Interesting how we ignored her on that one.

We never ate properly as kids. With little money to work with, and Mom's need for her cigarettes and love story magazines, we didn't have nourishing food. Fruit and vegetables were very rare. When Dad was home, Mom would prepare meat, potatoes and vegetables for him and there was always a dessert. We could smell the wonderful scents cooking and would get excited. Dad was always fed first and we were warned not to come near the table until he had left it. Most week nights he would eat by himself and on the weekends we ate together. I don't know if he was aware of the fact that we weren't being fed properly or if he chose to ignore the fact but every night we would wait for him to finish. We would hope that he wouldn't ask for seconds but some nights he did and on those occasions we got next to nothing. We were always told to keep our mouths shut. On holidays such as Christmas, we always had a big dinner and we would all sit down together. These were the times we looked forward to because it was a chance to fill our bellies.

When Dad was away at sea, we ate a lot of soup and peanut butter sandwiches.

We drank a lot of tea because that was Mom's favourite drink and because you didn't have to use a lot of milk in the tea. Milk was reserved for your cereal in the morning if you were lucky. Most morning's breakfast consisted of toast and whatever you could find to drink. Some days all we got for all 3 meals was toast because that was all Mom could afford. I could never understand why my friends didn't seem to be going without food like we were. Most families had the same number of kids and some you knew were really poor but they always seemed to have enough to eat. I guess some people knew how to make a dollar stretch farther than others and then again maybe it was just they had family to help them out. We didn't have any family close by to help so we did the best we could.

We never went to a dentist unless we were" dying with a tooth ache". There was no medical coverage for dentistry in those days and you had to pay for it unless you were lucky enough to be seen by the base dentist. The fee was taken out of the sailor's pay. I remember once having an abscessed tooth. Oh I thought the pain was going to kill me. Well I was wrong, the dentist who pulled the tooth was going to kill me, I was sure of it. I never went near another dentist after that until I was in my twenties. It hurt me so badly, I was afraid to go near another dentist. But it is one of my fears I am able to deal with.

I remember parties that Mom and Dad would hold in the apartment. We would be sent to bed or stay at a friend's house for the night. Most times we were home. They would party way into the night and most times we would be awake for most of it. On a few occasions Dad would come and get us and bring us to meet people. Most times though, we would get into trouble, even if we came out of our rooms to use the bathroom. When the party was over Mom and Dad would get into a fight about who was flirting with whom. These parties rarely ended with just going to bed. There always was a problem and the house was filled with tension.

Holidays and vacations were a nightmare. At Christmas time Dad would never give Mom money for shopping until the 23rd. She would then have to scramble to try and get stuff for us which was not an easy chore since she had to rely on buses. He would always tell us he was not going to go and get a tree. He wasn't putting one up. Then on the 23rd or 24th he would come in with one and we would have to hastily decorate it the best we could. There was no such thing as wanting something in particular such as a new doll or a new game. It wasn't going to happen because the stores would usually be sold out long before she got any money.

Easter wasn't any better. If we got a new outfit we were doing well. Sometimes we did and sometime we didn't. It wasn't because he didn't have any money; it was because he wouldn't part with it. If we needed anything at all we had to wait until he was drunk and then get the money out of him and go get what we needed before he could ask for the money back.

Holiday dinners were not festive. He would always criticize Mom about her cooking. He would go to the kitchen, insulting her and hollering that she "couldn't do anything right". We listened to this apprehensively and tried to help out where we could in order to reduce the tension. He would tell one of us to set the table as Mom didn't know how to set a proper table. Then after all this, we had to sit through dinner like we were one big happy family.

Vacations were a night mare. We always went to Windsor, Ontario to visit his family. We had to be up at 5am to be ready to hit the road for 6am. Nine times out of ten, we were never ready and we had hell to pay. It was always Mom's fault, never his. It didn't matter that he knew what we had to have with us. What camping gear, clothing, food, etc... He was the outdoors man, not us, but somehow we managed to get on the road. God forgive if you asked him to stop for a bathroom break. He would drive from Dartmouth, NS to New Brunswick before he would stop for lunch then continue to the Maine border and we would set up camp usually in New Hampshire for the night. Trying to set up camp was another headache because we were all girls and "we didn't know anything". Dad was the type of man who foolishly assumed that if he happened to know how to do a particular thing and you didn't, then you were, "a dummy and didn't know anything". We learned very quickly to be busy or disappear until he was done. Once the tent was set up then he would proceed to start cooking supper. By the time the meal was cooked and dishes cleaned up we were ready for bed knowing that we had to do it all over again the next day. It was supposed to be fun but it wasn't.

Then an enormous, life altering tragedy struck.

THE ACCIDENT

On Monday, May 22, 1961 my father left to go to sea. He was on the HMCS Haida and was to be gone for about 3 months. Dad had brought me back a couple of dresses from a previous trip to Holland and I was wearing one to school that day. I had turned seven years old in April and I was about to make my First Communion on Sunday May 27th. The Communion dress, veil, shoes and socks were bought and I was very excited about it. I was going to look beautiful and Mom was going to take pictures so Dad could see how pretty I was. The dress, from what I remember was white with short sleeves and covered in lace. The shoes were white and the socks had lace on them. The veil had a crown for the headpiece.

On the morning of May 23 everything was normal. Dad was gone, we left for school at 8:45 and got out for lunch at 12 noon and walked home. On that day, Mom was getting ready to go out somewhere and had put soup on the stove. I was the first one home and a knock came on the door. It was the boy downstairs wanting to know if they could borrow a cup of sugar. His family was one we usually borrowed from. It was approximately 12:15 and I told Mom I would get it.

I pushed a chair over to the stove (not knowing it was on) and proceeded to reach up into the cupboard to get a cup to put the sugar in. When I reached up, my dress hit the burner that was now showing red hot and my dress caught fire. I jumped off the chair and grabbed the dress and tried to smother it but that only made it worse as the dress was well starched and it spread fast. The boy ran from the door.

While I was busy trying to smother the fire, a boy my parents were looking after came in for lunch. He saw what was happening to me and started screaming "Mrs. Blaney, Mrs. Blaney "and I was hollering "Mom, Mom". She thought that we were fighting and didn't respond.

He ran out in fear and left me, and I continued to holler for Mom finally saying that I was on fire.

I put my hands on my face because the flames were now over my head and just stood there. I was paralyzed with fear. I couldn't move. I was screaming and crying. Our dog "Blackie" was running around and barking loudly. Mom finally came out of her room, took one look and screamed. I could see her panicked face through my fingers as the fire danced around me. She tried to keep the flames from my face and was looking for the fire extinguisher that was behind the door but it was covered with coats and she didn't see it. She was screaming now, calling out for help. She opened the door and ran me across the hall to the apartment next door. She threw open the door. The man in there was taken by surprise. He was just home from sea and jumped up and grabbed me and rolled me in a carpet. Everything happened so fast. At this point most of the tenants of the building had gathered at the landing. I remember seeing them standing there, their hands over their mouths in sheer shock. I was taken back to our apartment and a clean sheet was placed around me by the lady downstairs, Mrs. Cohen. She was trying to keep the draft off me. Wisely, she also tried to hold it out to keep it from touching me. She realized I was going into shock and administered water to me through an eyedropper. I have no idea where the eyedropper came from but I think her quick thinking may have saved my life. I was placed on a chair and Mrs. Cohen was holding the sheet around me when all of a sudden the firemen came through the door. The first fireman asked where the fire was. Neighbours that were now in the house, keeping my mother calm, told him the fire was out. They were now waiting on the ambulance. The second fireman came through the door, saw me and said, "Dear Jesus", and left. My mother ran in panic to the balcony and screamed "where is that ambulance? She's going to die, she's going to die." One of the neighbours slapped her, trying to bring her out of shock, and told her to calm down and to shut the balcony door. I remember saying in a very low voice (because I couldn't talk loud) that I wasn't going to die, I was just tired. Mrs. Cohen, the lady holding the sheet, kept talking to me and telling me not to go to sleep. She talked to me about my First Communion, and anything else that came to her mind. She was trying to keep me awake. I remember telling her, "My skin is black" and "Why am I so tired?" and "Daddy is going to be mad at me because I burned up the dress" and "Why is my skin falling off?"

It was now 1:15, an hour had passed and still there was no ambulance. Then someone heard it. The train whistle. There was a train that ran through the area every day between 12:30 and 1:00 and it was not unusual for it to stop on the tracks, cutting off the road into Shannon Park. The ambulance had not arrived because the train was in the way. A fireman ran out the door and from what I have been told, he drove up to the train conductor and had them separate the train and let the ambulance through. By now I was beginning to swell up. I don't remember much about the ambulance attendants except that they put me on a stretcher and put a red heavy blanket on me and strapped me down. That was the correct procedure as prescribed in those days. It was the worst thing they could have done because the wool blanket kept the heat in instead of allowing it to escape. So I kept burning while I was strapped on the stretcher.

I remember them carrying me down all those flights of stairs and the people crowding behind them. I could hear all their voices. My mother was still in a panic and the neighbours from our building were trying to get her to calm down before going to the hospital.

We finally reach the outside and other neighbours had gathered wondering who was going in the ambulance. I remember my best friend Ruby standing there holding a loaf of bread. When she saw it was me, she dropped the bread and ran into her apartment. I never saw her again for about six months.

The ambulance attendant was giving me oxygen and my mother and my sibling were up front with the driver. We lived in Dartmouth and had to go to Halifax to the Children's hospital. That required a drive through Dartmouth to the MacDonald Bridge and then through Halifax. It would take approximately a half hour drive normally but I have no idea how quick they got me there. I know the siren was going and the mask was on my face and I kept asking the man to turn off the siren as it was too loud and it was bothering me and I wanted that thing off my face because I didn't like the smell and he just kept talking to me and telling me the siren had to be on so they could get me there quickly and I needed to keep the mask on to help me breathe. I don't remember him doing anything else to me other than talking. I remember asking him to take off the blanket that I was too hot but he said he couldn't. My Mom kept turning around because she could hear the attendant hollering at me to stay awake. I remember vaguely telling him that I was "sleepy" and he kept telling me not to go to sleep, to keep talking to him. I don't remember anything upon arriving in the hospital. I don't know if I passed out but I am assuming that I did because the next thing I remember is being in a big room on another stretcher. All kinds of people were around me and there was a big light hanging from the ceiling. They were the emergency team on that day and they were the doctors and nurses that were trying to help me. I remember one nurse who kept talking to me and I asked her for something to drink. She asked a doctor who told her to give me a little bit and to watch for choking as I was swelling. I remember a doctor at the end of the table, at my feet, and he was hurting me and I started to cry and asked him to stop but I guess he couldn't hear me. The nurse put her ear down to me and I told her he was hurting me. She repeated it to the doctor who in turn told me he was sorry but he had to do this. What he was doing was putting intravenous lines and blood lines into the veins in my feet but I didn't know that until much later. They couldn't use my arms because they were burned. Getting fluids back into my body was imperative for survival and to ward off infection from the burnt skin.

I was burned over 70% of my body, from my knees up to my chin. I would later learn that Mrs. Cohen, the lady that held the sheet around me had sustained first degree burns to her face from the heat off my body and that my mother had burned her hands trying to keep the flames from my face. So between me covering my face and my mother trying to keep the flames from my face, my face was not burned. I had burns on my chin and a little up the side of my face and I had no hair and my eye lashes and brows were gone but the rest of my face was ok. But why was my skin black and falling off?

The emergency room was a whirl of doctors and nurses. The main doctor was shouting orders to the rest and they would respond. The doctor who was at the foot of the bed came to my side and told me he was Dr. Barton and he was going to take care of me. He said I was going to go to sleep now and he would see me when I woke up. I asked for my mother but he told me it was important that he look after me right now and I could see my mother when I woke up. I told him I had to be home by Saturday because I was making my First Communion on Sunday and I had to be there. He told me he would do his best to have me out by Saturday. This all happened very fast. Then he was back at my feet and I remember him saying to the team, "Are you ready?" and then everything went dark.

I realize now that at this point there was no pain. I remember feeling really hot and sleepy but no pain. This I am told was because my body was in shock and my nerve endings were severely damaged. The pain would soon follow. Pain that was unimaginable. Pain that is so severe that your mind shuts it off until you are ready to acknowledge it. The mind is a wonderful thing. It only allows you to remember what you can when you are ready for it

Now while all of this was going on with me in the emergency room, I found out that my mother was outside the door crying "my baby, my baby" and wanting to know what was happening with me. She was struggling with the staff and the nurse who was trying to calm her down discovered that my mother's hands were burned and needed to be treated. My mother refused treatment and remained hysterical. In spite of this, they managed to tend to her hands, sedate her and take her to the Victoria General Hospital as they realized that she was going into shock. She was admitted to the hospital and they had to wait until she had some control over herself to see how extensive her burns were. My mother cannot take penicillin, and they had given her a shot for infection and she reacted to it. With everything that she had been through, she needed to be admitted and watched. While she was in this mental and physical state, she was told that I probably would not survive. The burns were deep and extensive and she should prepare herself for the worst.

One of the neighbours ran to the church to get the base priest who was dispatched to my bedside. He called the Military Base Officer who had an emergency call placed to the ship to inform my father what had happened. The priest later told me that my father was told that I was not going to survive and that the Navy had instructed the ship to turn around and bring him in. They were not far off the coast and they had him back in the next day. I later had this account confirmed by a newspaper article I found about my accident and a statement about the ship being brought back in. Dad had to contend with me in one hospital and my mother in another. From what was told me, my mother was released once my father got home.

I finally woke up in the old Halifax Children's Hospital. There was no family there and I was scared and I had no idea what was happening to me or why. I was confused. All I knew was that I was in a room. The room had two beds in it and the door was closed. There was a nurse with me and there were all kinds of bottles hanging on the bed attached to my ankles. Tubes had been inserted into my nose and throat. There was a cradle over me keeping the sheets off my skin and I was covered in bandages from head to foot. There was a window in the room and it had yellow curtains. I looked at them and started screaming and crying and pointing to the curtains because I thought they were on fire. My screaming sounded more like a bad asthma attack and wheezing, due to smoke inhalation. The nurse jumped up and pulled the curtains down telling me that everything was all right, it was just the colour I was seeing, the fire was out and I was going to be fine. She put something in the intravenous and it put me back to sleep. I don't know how long this went on but I still had not seen any of my family. I know there was always a nurse in the room with me. The first 48 hours of recovery are absolutely critical. Blood pressure must be kept up, vital signs constantly monitored and the much needed fluids put back into the body as quickly as your body is spilling them out. I remember nurses coming in about every four hours to change my bandages. In those days it was just saline and gauze that made up the bandages and it was sheer torture to have them removed. These bandages were just laid on my body but would stick like glue in my charred and dead skin. I would scream and cry. Some nurses cried with me and tried to reassure me, but it was so painful. This would go on and on and by the time they were finished I was exhausted from screaming.

In 1961, the technique of putting people into induced comas had not been developed. I had to suffer through this with only antibiotics and pain meds to get me through. The problem with pain meds is that they wear off and the body requires more. But more was not to be for a child and much suffering was endured. I had little to no voice from the smoke inhalation and the burns on my neck. I could only make sounds in a whisper.

When my father arrived home he blamed my mother for what had happened. My mother never got over that. They were told that IF I survived, which was unlikely, I would be in for a long recovery. There wasn't much they could do for me but try to keep me comfortable. If I survived there were a number of scenarios that could come into play. There was the possibility of immobility. The possibility of never walking again. The possibility of brain damage from the smoke. The possibility of nerve damage. Finally, there was the possibility that they wouldn't have to deal with any of that as the possibility of me surviving were very slim. People with less degree and less coverage than I had, typically did not make it.

It was 3 days before my father saw me. I don't know if that was the first time I remember seeing him, but I don't think so. I believe that I was heavily sedated for a period of time to help with the pain and I was in and out of consciousness so my first memory of him being there would be sometime later. I do remember them telling me later on in life that they couldn't figure out why I had a black blanket on me so the debriding had not been done yet. (Debriding is when your skin is washed, the dead skin is peeled off and blisters broken by using tweezers. It is extremely painful.) When I was awake for longer periods there was always a nurse with me. They would try to make me comfortable, talk to me and try to be as cheery as possible. I became depressed and unresponsive which I'm told is normal after an accident like that but I cannot tell you the pain. How anyone can survive that must have a strong will to live because it is the most unbearable pain imaginable. To have your whole body burning and paining all at the same time is something that words really can't describe. The nurses and doctors wore surgical gowns from head to toe so you didn't know anyone; all you could see were their eyes. Their hands were gloved and if I touched them, trying to stop them from hurting me, they would have to leave the room, re gown and glove and start again. Most of the time there would be two nurses doing it, trying to get it done faster, but it was always so painful. I believe that Debbie the seven year old child died that day of the fire and that Debbie the Victim emerged, fighting for her life.

I remember the first time I saw my parents. They were gowned and gloved also, as the room had to be kept sterile. I didn't know them at first. They both held my hands and told me how sorry they were for this happening to me. All I did was cry. There was nothing more I could do. I couldn't communicate with them at all because of all the tubes and I thought Dad would be mad at me for ruining the dress he bought me. Mom had a hard time looking at me. She felt so guilty. I could see the pain in her eyes. The nurse was always with me, she explained to my parents that I may not remember them being there as I was heavily sedated. I don't know how long they stayed but I do remember the doctor coming in and asking to speak with Mom and Dad privately. They kissed me good bye and said they would see me the next day. They came back the next day and Dad explained that he had to go into the hospital himself for a little while but he would be back to see me as soon as possible. Mom would continue to come over by herself until he got back.

I found out later that they needed one of my parents to donate their skin to me to be used as a covering to help get my blood cells going. It was decided that Dad would be the better candidate as Mom had been through enough with her hands and they needed it done right away. Dad was admitted to the

Stadacona Hospital where they literally peeled the skin from his legs to use as a covering for me. This skin would die off me but would help to produce the necessary blood cells that I needed to survive. Unfortunately for my Dad, Stadacona was not used to dealing with this procedure and they left the bandages on him too long and they had to put him back to sleep to get the bandages off. He claims it was one of the most painful surgeries he ever had to endure. Welcome to my world.

The skin was transferred over to the Children's Hospital. I was taken up to surgery and the skin was placed over the burns as a covering. The burns were wrapped and the skin left there. Over time, a horrible stink arose from the smell of the new skin dying off combined with the smell of burned flesh. After a few days the dead skin was removed by debriding and the next lot of Dad's skin put on. This was done about 3 times and each time seemed more painful than the last.

Dad returned for visits and found me to be sullen and quiet. Upon inquiring as to my state, he was told that I had been going downhill and the outcome was not looking good. Unless they could find a way to get me to respond and start fighting there wasn't much more they could do. They also informed him that I had doctors and nurses around the clock doing whatever they could but my survival was very uncertain.

I was being fed by intravenous and receiving blood. I couldn't take anything by mouth because of my throat being swollen. I had tubes in my nose and in my throat, just tubes everywhere. They would take tubes out, hoping I would respond on my own but then end up putting them back in. It just seemed to be a lot of pain. I had to sleep on my back. I couldn't roll over. I was hurting so bad all the time. My body was one huge blister. Several times I was taken to surgery so they could break the blisters and do major debriding.

The nurses would come and move me over to the other bed so they could change the bed I was in. Everything they did was unmerciful pain. They would slide me onto a stretcher and then slide me onto the other bed and then the same routine back. They always gave me something for pain before they would move me and then I would sleep when they were done.

Dr. Barton was one of the most fatherly doctors a patient could ask for. He was so kind to me, always referring to me as his little girl. He would tell me that they had to do something to me and then he would come in gowned up with other doctors. This was usually a debridement and I would scream all through it. First they would put me in a tub bath to soak my skin. The tub was a regular tub and they would wash it out with sterile soap and then tape a sterile sheet to the inside and then put me in it. Then they would take me back to my room and the debridement would start. I don't know how they could keep going with me screaming. Mom and Dad would beg them to stop and they finally had to tell Mom and Dad not to come over during those times. It had to be done to ward off infection and it was never going to be a pleasant thing. I would hear my mother begging him to stop. She would be crying and I would be begging him to stop and the circle kept going until they stopped coming. Debridement is like being peeled alive. The pain was so intense that I would pass out. Fortunately today they put patients into a coma but I had to suffer through it and suffer I did. The hospital would inform my parents that they would be doing a procedure during a particular time and they would stay home.

My limbs started to shrivel up and soon I couldn't straighten my legs or my arms. They would take me up to surgery and put me to sleep and straighten my limbs by putting casts on them. I was a human cast with only an opening to go to the bathroom. They had inserted a catheter right from the beginning so it was just the other end to worry about. After a few days the smell was unbearable. There were green soft spots on the cast and the smell was rank. I complained all the time about the smell and the nurses addressed it with the doctors. The smell was being caused by the oozing from the burns and this pus would pool on my skin and under the cast and just sit on top of my skin. Eventually the cast would develop green spots which were soft spots in the cast from the oozing. They would again take me up to surgery and take off the casts and clean me up. My limbs would be perfectly straight for about five minutes. As soon as I bent my arm to see it, that was it, it was back in the bent up position. They would leave me alone for a few days and then I would go back up and have the casts put back on. The reason for the casts was to try to stretch out my skin. It didn't work and was pure torture for me.

Miss MacDonald was the nurse who was with me the most. I believe her job was to try to get me to respond to her in any way possible. She would start most mornings by calling me a sour puss. I would respond by fighting with her and this routine would become habit. I loved Miss MacDonald. She did everything for me but also started making me help myself. On her days off I was miserable. I only wanted her.

I had a doll, a black walking doll that I got the previous Christmas and Mom brought it into the hospital thinking that it might cheer me up. The hospital washed down the doll and put her into a hospital gown and put her in the bed next to me. When it was time for my dressing changes, one of the nurses thought it would be a good idea to bandage up the doll the same way I was. I thought it was great that she was just like me. One day a black nurse came in the room and started talking to me and then she started talking to the doll. She said she thought the doll was another person in the room. I laughed and laughed at this. I thought it was so funny. I think this was one of the first times that I had a hearty laugh. It brightened my spirits for a bit. Every time that nurse was on duty, I would remember that moment and she also made a point of continuing with her conversations with me and then the doll. Those nurses knew what they were doing. I sure admire them for their dedication and their humanity.

Somewhere in here, I believe it was July or August and I was still on the critical list, my grandparents arrived from Windsor, Ontario. I wasn't sure who they were as I had not seen them for a while and they were wearing the gowns, masks and gloves. My father had to tell me who they were and I really don't remember knowing them. My grandfather came over to me and was talking to me, hoping I was feeling better and that I wasn't hurting too much. I remember seeing my grandmother sitting in a chair in the corner. She never came near me. I don't know why. Maybe it was shock at how I looked. She never even kissed me good bye. As they were leaving Dad explained to me that all four of them were going away for a few days. I remember crying and asking him not to leave me but they went any way. So here I was, on the critical list and my parents go off on a vacation with my grandparents. I was totally alone. My siblings weren't old enough to visit me. The hospital rules were that you had to be 16 and older in order to visit. The only people I saw were neighbours in the building who came by to see me. One woman in particular was Mrs. Cohen. She was the woman who held the sheet around me and fed me by eyedropper. She would come by as often as she could and when Mom and Dad went away, she came every day. The only other person who came was our priest, Father Pelletier. Mrs. Cohen always came with a gift for me. It didn't matter what it was, she never came empty handed. She felt that it put a smile on my face and that was all she wanted to see. When I was able to eat, she always brought me treats, really rich treats because they needed to get some fat on my body. She made the best goodies.

Father Pelletier knew I was upset about missing my First Communion, so he arranged for me to do it in the hospital. They allowed Mom to put my veil on my head, but that was all and I made my First Communion in the hospital bed. Father

Pelletier gave me a beautiful set of ice blue rosary beads that I will cherish forever. He also gave me two wall plaques, one with a Guardian Angel overlooking two children crossing a bridge and the other of Jesus knocking on a door. I still have those plaques today. From what I have been told, I made my First Communion quite soon after the accident. Once they had me stable, they did it right away. Father Pelletier would come by every day to see me and pray over me. Between him and Mrs. Cohen I was being looked after.

While Mom and Dad were away with my grandparents, my sister Susanne came to see me. She gowned up and was talking to me when a nurse came in and asked her how old she was. She was just 15 and the nurse had to ask her to leave. I cried after her but the nurse wouldn't relent and I again went down-hill. I told Dr. Barton what happened and he had a call made for my sister to come back. They allowed her in after that. I still can't believe that my parents went on vacation with me still on the critical list. According to my sisters, my mother didn't want to go but Dad forced her to, telling her it would do her good to get away from the stress. They went to Cape Breton, on the Cabot Trail, which was one of my mother's favourite places. She always said that Cape Breton and Newfoundland reminded her of home, Scotland. She told me later in life that she didn't want to go on that trip, but what was done was done. I know I felt all alone. I had neighbours and Priests but not my Mommy and Daddy. I thought that I must have done something really bad for them to leave me behind. I guessed that Dad was mad at me for burning up the dress. When my parents returned, it was as if they had done nothing wrong.

I eventually began eating soft foods and the higher in calories the better. Dad would bring me a milkshake every night and would ask me what I wanted to eat. Occasionally I would ask for a hamburger but the most I ate was Post Alpha-Bits cereal. That was my favourite and the hospital had orders to give it to me any time I asked. I think Alpha –Bits may have had a hand in saving my life as well.

My room was rapidly filling up with gifts and cards from everyone we knew. Dad would have to take stuff home at the end of a couple of weeks because the room was so full. There was everything imaginable, mostly stuffed animals and religious tokens. There were hundreds of get well cards. I tried to salvage as many of the cards as I could but out of the hundreds, I have only about 60 in a scrap book. I was now completely spoiled. When doctor's orders are to give her whatever she wants, I got it. I remember when Dad was allowed to bring a TV into the room for me, I was in heaven.

As time went on, they started doing physical therapy. It was mostly stretching and again I would scream. The person for this was Miss Crosby. As soon as I saw her coming I would begin to cry. I knew what she was going to do to me. She would put her hand under my elbow and with the other hand would pull my arm down. There was a band (skin that shrinks in certain parts of the body that forms a tightness of thick skin) that had formed in the area where my arm bands and she had to stretch it out on both arms. My body would conform to any position trying to get her to stop. She would do one arm and then the next and then she would stretch out my legs. Again a large band had formed between each leg and she would stretch these out. All of this was pure torture for me and again when I saw her coming I would begin to cry. There were several bands on my chest and neck and across my belly that would have to be released at some point. After several weeks of this the bands started to break down and bleed and it was decided that I would have to have some skin grafts.

Around this time Dr. Barton thought it would be a good idea to have me taken to the roof for some fresh air. This was all done with me covered completely until we reached the roof. This was where the doctors and nurses would go for a break.

Once there they would open up the sheets over the cradle and I was left there for what was supposed to be no more than an hour. On this particular day, it was beautiful outside and I remember all the doctors and nurses who would come over and talk to me and ask me if I remembered what had happened to me. I eventually fell asleep and when I woke up I asked a doctor for a drink. He got me the drink and asked me what floor I was on and I had no idea. I also had no idea that I was now sunburned on top of my burns. He called around and found out where my room was and proceeded to take me back to the floor. Yes, I was sunburned and my doctor was having a fit. The nurse was not supposed to leave me alone and somehow she had forgotten that I was still up there. There was a price to be paid for her forgetfulness. I think she may have been transferred or fired as I never saw her again. Now they had to get the sunburn under control and I had to go through the pain again. They heavily soaked my skin and kept it cool and sedated me again. Within a few days things were back to normal but I never went to the roof again.

After I was taken off the critical list, my parent's visits became staggered. My mother could not drive and had to depend on buses to get back and forth and on the neighbours to keep an eye on my sisters. My father could drive, but he went back to work and would drop in when he could. There were days when I saw no one and it was very lonely. Mrs. Cohen would come by as often as she could and would drive Mom over at times but she had a husband and a family as well and could not come over all the time. A few times Mom had to bring my sisters with her and they had to wait downstairs in the lobby. Mom made the suggestion to one of the nurses that perhaps I could be moved to the other bed so I could look out the window and see them. This proved to be very therapeutic and it became a way for people to be able to see me, although it was only my face in the window.

The physiotherapist came to see me and told me they were going to stand me up on my feet and teach me how to walk. I remember telling her that I was seven years old and I knew how to walk. She tried to explain to me that I would not be able to walk due to being in bed so long and because of the condition of my skin. She had me sit on the edge of the bed and told me to slide to the end of the bed. Her and her assistant would hold me up. Feeling confident and independent, I slid to the end of the bed and tried to stand on my own. I was going to show them that I could walk. Well, before they could catch me, I fell flat on the floor. They were concerned that I had hurt myself but I didn't. I just could not believe that I couldn't walk. They helped me up to a sitting position and waited a few minutes and then they helped me stand up. Standing on my two feet proved to be very difficult indeed. The bands in my legs were constricting me from standing up straight. I couldn't move my legs at all on my own and they had to push my feet in front of me until I got the hang of it. We only did this for about 20 minutes and I was very discouraged that I was unable to walk on my own. They praised me for trying and said they would be back the next day to try again. We did this day after day. They would hold me up and I would try moving my legs. Over time it got easier but they could not let go of me as I had no balance as yet. My whole body was reshaped from the burns and I could not stand up straight but they kept encouraging me. One day they brought me down to the physiotherapy department. They told me they were going to see if I could hold myself up on the parallel bars. They helped me up to the bars and stood on each side of me. I remember holding on for dear life and attempting to walk. It took a few times of moving arms and legs at the same time in order to keep off the floor but I finally got my coordination together and started to walk on my own. Then one day when they took me down, my parents were there as well as Dr. Barton. They wheeled me up to the bars and I stood and walked down the bars with no help. Dr. Barton was smiling a huge smile and Mom was crying and Dad caught me at the end. I was so proud of myself. I could walk. This whole process took about a month or so and I was improving daily.

I had been there about five months and the door to my room had always been kept shut. Finally they opened the door so I could see out. Other kids could not come into my room but I was able to talk to people in the doorway. It seemed like such a small thing, but it was a huge and wonderful thing. Five months behind a closed door. I could hear people out there all the time and now I could be part of it. After several more physio appointments, I was finally allowed to leave my room. I would hold on to the wall and walk the hallway and turn around and walk back. But there was a new problem, a new form of torture that was beginning to happen to me. It started slowly but had gotten to great strength and was as irritating as the pain. It was keeping me awake and making me very restless and cranky. I now had the healing ITCH. An itch so unbearable that the only thought I could hold in my head was to scratch. For me that was dangerous because it would tear my skin and all they could do for me was put me in baking soda baths and cover me with vaseline jelly. I was plastered in it and it would only hold for so long. I had to be kept cool and some nights it meant a trip to the bath in the middle of the night to try and settle the itch down.

I was getting better and it looked like I might even get to go home soon. I had been here for six and a half months and Dr. Barton kept his promise. He sent me home on a Saturday in December with the understanding that I would be back for another long stay after Christmas.

My siblings were being looked after by the neighbours and they saw very little of their parents for a long time. They grew to resent me because of all the time it took away from the family, them being separated from Mom and Dad and things that their parents should have attended to for them at school, were not met because they had to be at the hospital for Debbie. They had no idea what was happening to me or for that matter what was being done to me. All they knew was that Debbie had burned and now Mom and Dad were with her all the time. They had no idea that this injury was permanent. They thought I would be in the hospital for a few days and then I would come home. Why was it taking so long? The doctors can fix things so how come it was taking them so long to fix Debbie. It wasn't fair to them. And they would ask Mom and Dad why and they had no answers for them.

NOTE: Upon my sister Susanne reading this part, she advised me that the resentment issue was not true; however I explained to her that this was what Dad had told me and what I had believed all these many years.

THE HOMECOMING

I was very excited to be going home. Dad had come to the hospital the night before and had taken home a car full of gifts. Now all there was to do was get the instructions from the nurses' station and we could leave. Dad was advised that VON (Victorian Order of Nurses) would be in daily to help with the dressings and the medications I needed. He was advised that I would have to take baking soda baths on a daily basis to help with the itch and, of course, the Vaseline. I looked around me and all the nurses that had looked after me were there to see me off. I clung to Miss MacDonald and started to cry. She told me to get going before I made her cry but I could see she already was. I had no idea how things had changed for me but this was going to be the first day of a very long, rough road in addition to the physical pain, I was now going to learn how cruel children can be.

The first shocker for me was that my parents had moved from the building that I had been burned in. Shannon Park was like row housing of apartment buildings. The buildings were all in sections and each section had its own playground in the center. My accident occurred in building 8J, apartment 6, and third floor. They had moved down to the next building, 8H, apartment 3 to the first floor because I could not climb the stairs. There was an advantage to this because 8J was a 2 bedroom apt and 8H was a 3 bedroom. They needed the extra bedroom for me.

My father picked me up from the hospital in the morning and we proceeded home. I was very excited and talked a mile a minute. The biggest surprise for me was that all the people in the buildings were either outside waiting for me or on their balconies. They were clapping and hollering "Welcome Home", I was trying to walk by myself. My father was holding me by the elbow because I was still bent over like a little old lady but I wanted to do it myself. I think a lot of people were shocked at seeing me this way, not having any idea what to expect. But I was determined I was going to walk alone and asked Dad to let go of me. He was hesitant but he did let go and with the tiny steps that I could only take, I took what seemed liked the longest walk in my life. But I did it.

The apartment seemed like a castle, although they are really very small. After being in one room for six and a half months it seemed like a palace. The apartment was alive with well-wishers and the curious but all I wanted to see was my friend Ruby. She had come to the hospital several times with my Mom and I would wave to her from the window and now we could be together. I was not allowed to do a lot but just having her there was comfort enough for me. I wanted her to stay forever but it wasn't long before I grew tired from all the excitement and Mom had to send people home so I could rest. I didn't want to rest in my mind but my body was telling me otherwise. When I first got home I was rooming with my sister in the larger bedroom but soon after they had to switch me and put my sisters together because I was keeping them up all night with my scratching. The itch was horrific and the only solution at that time was the baths. The first night home Mom was trying to get me to take the bath and I wanted no part of it. I had had enough of this routine and as far as I was concerned they couldn't make me. Mom tried everything and I resisted. I was crying that I didn't want to go in the bath and Mom knew that it was important to set down the rules right away. She had to call in the VON nurse who got fed up with my antics and put me in the tub, clothes and all. She proceeded to take my clothes off in the tub. I was not a happy camper. Mrs. Cohen lived in the next building 8J, apartment 3. Because of the way the buildings were laid out, like an L shape, my bedroom window was very close to her kitchen and she could hear all the crying that I was doing and the goings on and came over to find out what was wrong. She helped the VON nurse with me and my Mom stayed out in the kitchen. Her nerves were frazzled with me and she didn't know how to cope with it. Another neighbour made her a cup of tea and talked with her while I was being tended to. After the bath, they applied the Vaseline and I soon fell asleep from exhaustion. That night was horrible, I kept waking up with the itch and I was driving my sister crazy with the continuous scratching. Mom kept applying the Vaseline but the room was too warm for me and it increased the itching. I remember getting out of the bed and curling up on the floor. It was the coolest place in the house. After a few nights of this and me not cooperating, Mrs. Cohen stepped in again with an idea that was going to turn things around for everyone as far as the baths went. With me fighting against it so much at home, Mrs. Cohen would bring over a treat for me if I would get in the bath. She decided that maybe the better way to do it was to take the bath over at her house. It would be a less stressful way for me to get done what had to be done but there would be a bonus in it for me because she would make me homemade milk shakes plus she always had treats. There was also the fact that her husband "Tiny", was almost 7 feet tall. When he spoke I listened. After my baths, I would sit with him on the couch and he would talk to me and their son Brian. Brian was 16, the same age as my sister Susanne. The plan worked out for everyone, except that I was still driving myself and everyone at home crazy with the itching.

My friend Ruby would still come by after school but I soon realized she wasn't staying as long and after a while she didn't come as often. She drifted away, but it was understandable. I still couldn't attend school, so my work was sent home to me. School had resumed in September and I was now in grade 2 but I hadn't attended yet. In addition, my limbs were still bent up and I was very restricted in what I could do. So, as a play mate, I wasn't much fun. I couldn't run, skip or play as a normal seven year old girl would.

THE SURGERIES

After my homecoming I was back in the hospital to start the grafting process sometime in January or February and I was again in hospital for quite a while.

The surgeries started first with my right arm. I was not told that they would peel skin off my back and graft it to my burnt areas. When I awoke I felt a sharp unrelenting pain from my back. They used the skin from my back for the graft since this area was not burned. My back hurt worse than my arm. I couldn't get comfortable at all. They had my arm hanging on a pole, straight up in the air. This really hurt because the blood pooled in the bottom of my arm. I kept trying to put the pillow under my arm to rest it on but I got caught every time and finally after 2 days they put it down. I don't know what anyone was thinking but that had to be one of the most inhumane things anyone can do to another person. You try keeping your arm straight up in the air for hours and see if you can do it. I bet not. Again I was heavily sedated to try and keep me comfortable. Any movement was difficult for me. I would try and be brave but at seven brave doesn't come naturally. Scared is the natural reaction and I was scared silly.

My back felt as though it was burning. I thought I was on fire all over again and I had to be reassured that this was not what happened. They tried to explain to me what they did in terms that I could understand but I didn't understand. I couldn't understand why I was hurting so much and why this wasn't going away. I was in a hospital and I had a lot of doctors and nurses but this still wasn't going away. Why was this happening to me?

After the first skin graft healed, they decided to do the left arm. I went through the exact same thing only this time they took the skin from my behind. Many, many years later I was able to jokingly say that I'm the only person who can kiss their own behind. Having the first layer of your skin peeled away is like a burn all over again. It has the feeling of a huge paper cut. It is very, very painful. They used what is called "scarlet red" as a bandage for the "donor site" This was like a piece of red felt that stuck to the wound like glue. When the doctor felt it was on long enough, about a week, they would take it off and let the air at it. They would soak and soak this and have to pull at it gradually until they got it off. I would beg them to slow down, often they would give me a shot of something to help me along, but the pain was excruciating. When all was said and done it was good to have the use of my arms back. Now it was time for the more physical, physical therapy to start. They started by slowly sitting me up for short periods of time. Having been bed ridden for so long, I had no strength in my body at all. Even sitting up in the bed required me to be blocked in with pillows because I would slump over. It was not unusual for the nurse to come in and find me hanging on the bed rail. When I slumped over it was very difficult for me to reach the buzzer for help. During all of this the door to my room was still closed. When I was sitting up, it was discovered that I probably would not be able to stand straight until they did a few releases on my body. There were several bands, as I stated earlier, across my chest and stomach that prevented me from being able to hold myself up. A further complication was the fact that my underarms were fused together and constricting me. On my chest, the left breast had completely inverted and the nipple on my right breast was gone. The left side had formed a band over to the right side and would pull with the slightest movement of my arms. There were also crisscross bands across my stomach which wouldn't budge at all. So it was decided that I would have to undergo more releases. The surgeries would be on going for a number of years but nobody expected it to last for over 40 years. Nobody

THE EXPERIENCE

Dear Reader, I want to remind you that I was only a seven year old little girl. That I was about to make my First Communion when the experience happened to me. I told the doctor that I had to be home, he nodded and then he put me to sleep.

It was very peaceful. There was no noise, only silence. There was no pain. Someone seemed to be calling me. There was a warm glow all around me. I felt safe. I wasn't afraid for some reason. I had been taught to be afraid of the unknown but for some reason I wanted to go to this light. This glow that was around me. There were no hallways, or speed of light movement, it was just there. This light is like nothing that we have here on earth. It is a brilliance that does not hurt your eyes but you can't really describe it. I remember a man, and three ladies. The ladies seemed to be floating, their feet not touching on to anything. It wasn't the ground as we know it, nor was it a cloud but it seemed to be both. The ladies were the angels as we have been taught by religion but I saw no wings. They just hovered, their gowns flowing, colors unimaginable. The man was Jesus, somehow I knew this. He was the most beautiful person I had ever seen and he had his arms out stretched to me. He appeared to be sitting and his robe was a beautiful blue and he wore no shoes. His hair was long and wavy, a cross between a blonde and dark brown. There was a glow all around them and I believe that is why I can't determine what his hair color was because it was both. He spoke without moving his mouth, as if he had telepathy, told my mind what I wanted to hear and I spoke back to him without words. He said "Come to me my child" and I was drawn to him. He cradled me in his arms. "Would you like to stay here with me?" I wanted to stay with him, it was so peaceful. At this point I was wrapped in his arms and he was just holding me. He told me that he knew that I was suffering. I told him that I don't feel anything wrong with me and that I would like to stay with him but I was making my First Communion on Sunday and I wanted my Mommy and she would be very mad at me if I didn't show up. He smiled at me and told me that he would help me along this journey. He was still holding me on his lap, like a mother holds her newborn infant, and the angels were staying to the side of him and behind him. I didn't understand what he is telling me because I didn't see anything wrong with me. He told me that I will remember being with him and that I will question what has happened to me and that someday I will understand all of this. He told me that it is time for me to leave him now and that the angels will show me the way and to remember that he loves me. I told him that I loved him too. It was so natural to tell him that. The angels moved to my side and extended their hands pointing to me to return to the light. The light was fading. It was not as bright as before and as I walked through it, I turned and he was smiling at me and encouraging me to return and that we would meet again. I walked on and the light got dimmer and dimmer and then it was gone... I awoke in a room and in so much pain.

I was seven years old. I had no idea of near death experiences or out of body experiences. I was told that I had expired for a brief period of time but that they were able to resuscitate me. This must have been when this happened. The amazing thing about this is that I can remember it like it was yesterday but I cannot give you a face to this man... The mystery of Jesus will remain a mystery. When I think about this I can picture him but

I cannot put it on paper for the words to describe him will not come to me.

Debbie the 7 year old child died on May 23, 1961 and Debbie the burn victim emerged to fight the battle of a lifetime, and to somehow win the battle and become a survivor.

LIFE IN SHANNON PARK

The years ahead of me were very difficult especially where we were living on a naval base. People who knew me would try to help me but I was in the hospital so much it was hard to make friends. People would come and go, being drafted to different areas all the time. For the newcomers, they had no idea what had happened to me and life was very cruel.

When I first got home from the hospital, people were kind to me. They felt sorry for me but they had no idea what kind of pain I was in. After a while it became boring and was time for them move on to something else. But I couldn't move on to something else because I was trapped in this body. This body that was so scared and horrible to look at. I was constantly in bandages and there were nurses coming and going from the house. I would keep myself covered up in long sleeves and pants or long skirts because I didn't want anyone to see the burns. But in the summer when it was hot, I had to wear shorts and short sleeves because the itch would drive me crazy and I would overheat. It seemed that I could not control my body temperature at all. In the summer I was too hot and would have to shower or bath, 2 or 3 times a day to try and cool myself. In the winter I couldn't stay warm.

I soon learned that life for me was going to be very different from my friends or from my sisters for that matter. They were all dating and doing things that I could not do and thus it was the beginning of my shutting down from real life and staying in the house away from people and away from the hurtful remarks. In Shannon Park it was very easy to want to be part of something. One just had to look out the window; there was always someone you knew outside. They would be playing marbles, skipping, or playing baseball, or hide and seek or just sitting on a swing. There was always someone. I would try to be included but no one ever wanted me on their team because I was too slow. If we played hide and seek, I was always" it" because they could easily out run me. It was a terrible realization to finally understand that I was not really wanted in these games. It was even more hurtful to hear the cruel remarks, some heartless kids would make. So bit by bit, I started to stay away.

My self-esteem was being shattered on a regular basis even in our own apartment. Every time my father would take me somewhere or a newcomer would come to the house, he would put me on display, "show them your burns Debbie". I would be humiliated and embarrassed, again and again.

After my accident my parents had applied for adoption and when I was due to come home in April of 1962 from the second bout in the hospital, the baby was born. Upon my release from the hospital my father made a phone call to the Orphanage and arrange for me to see the baby. He was on the phone for a while and then we went to see him. I was really excited about having a baby brother and when we got there I chatted up a storm and they brought the baby to us. Mom and Dad were holding him and I wanted to hold him but my body was to weak and I think they were afraid I would drop him, so I just sat there and admired my new brother. This was supposed to be just a visit for me to meet my new brother but somehow when we left the visit, Eric was with us and now we were a family of six. At first it was very exciting to have a baby but I soon realized I wasn't the baby anymore and he was getting all the attention and I didn't like that. I had the normal jealousies of a young child and we grew up together, a six year difference in age and as he got older, a pain in the butt for me.

Life was not easy for us. Dad continued to run around on Mom and we paid the price with her abuse. Even little Eric was not spared. Incredibly, Dad started taking Eric to his girlfriend's home. When they returned, the first moment Mom got him alone she would start drilling him about where they were. He was too young to understand any of this and my sister stepped in and took care of Eric as much as possible. Poor Eric would get a spanking because he didn't know where he had been or who Dad was with. We all lived it, and as kids we tried to look out for each other but sometimes we were too late to avoid the storm.

As time went on I became very secluded and then I met a girl (Linda S.) who lived just a few houses from me. She was friends with the girl downstairs in the basement apartment (Linda D.) in my building and they started inviting me along with them. I think I was eleven or twelve years old. I developed a friendship with them for as long as we remained living there. I think it would have been about 2-3 years that we were all together. But over time, things changed. The girl downstairs and her family were transferred to the west coast and then my father retired from the military and we had to leave the military apartments. The other girl remained in the Park for a while and I would meet up with her from time to time but life moved on and we fell away from each other for many years. Many years later, as luck would have it, I was in Sobeysgrocery store in Sackville and I saw a woman who looked like Linda S's mother. I approached her and asked her if she was indeed Linda's mother and she said yes. I gave her my phone number and asked her to give it to Linda. A few days later Linda called me and we got together. We still get together when we can and it's nice to know that someone was there for you and you didn't even realize it until later in life. I laugh when I think of some ·

of the things we did. We never got into any serious trouble but we soon got known for hanging out in different hallways of other buildings especially on Sunday mornings. Our parents would send us out to church and instead of going to church we would hang in a building close to the church and smoke cigarettes. When it was close to church getting out we would go in the church and look around to see who was there and find out what the sermon was about. We could then tell our parents what was going on and they had no idea we weren't there.

There was always something to do in the Park and many people to do it with. Unfortunately for me, I watched most of this from a window or on the side lines by myself. I remember the toboggan rides on the hills where they had to literally smack into a building to stop. I remember the ice skating on the pond, the pool, and the endless games of red rover, tag, marbles, and "Teen Town" in the school gym. I remember the jetty boat and the store down by the jetty, the mail up in the building on the top of the hill and the nurse station, the commissionaires, the nuns on Sundays from Mount St. Vincent, the communion walks around the park when you were making your First Communion. In the summer there were recreation programs and trips to McNab's Island for swimming. We were in our own community; we didn't have to go anywhere else to have some fun. Everything was provided for us, even our schooling. When I meet up with people today or chat on the internet with other people who lived there, I listen to all the wonderful memories of the fun times they had and most of the memories are the same just with different people.

But Shannon Park was not a fun place for me. I tried to participate in things but was soon put down for it and made fun of so I would pull back. I didn't know what I had done for people to dislike me so much, but life for me became cold and I was shut out and made fun of and name called and told that I was just plain ugly. People started calling me names like "Crispy

Critter, French Fry, Burns, and Fried Blaney". My self- esteem hit the bottom floor.

I remember when the recreation center opened a pool. It was an outdoor pool and everyone was waiting to get in. There were so many kids, that a time limit had to be imposed. We would wait for about a half hour to get in. When we finally got in we had a half hour to swim. We then got out and back in line and you did this over and over all day. I wanted to do this with everyone else but that proved to be a big mistake for me. I waited in line with all the others and then it was my turn, I took off my shorts and top as I had my swim suit on under my clothes and immediately started to get stared at. I tried not to let that bother me and I proceeded to the pool and got in. Several people moved away from me and told me not to come where they were. I asked them why and they made remarks about my ugly, diseased body. They started to make fun of the way my body looked and within a few minutes I was crying. I got up out of the pool to get dressed and many remarks about my skin and looks were hollered behind me. They told me not to come back to the pool. I was not wanted. I was too ugly. I left the pool and went home. To this day I will not put on a bathing suit. What self- esteem I had left was shattered.

When Dad retired from the military we had to go house hunting. I was so looking forward to moving from there and at the same time I was scared to death. I was hoping this would be a new start for me with people who would give me a chance and accept me for who I was. I was about to find out that it didn't matter where I lived. When it came to me and my burns I didn't have a bloody chance.

THE MOVE

March 1967, we moved to Middle Sackville, Nova Scotia in a big 2 storey house on the Old Sackville Road. When we first got there I wondered what in the world I did to deserve this, as we were in the middle of nowhere. This was the country and I was used to city life. There were no buses out here. The telephone was a party line and to call my friends in Dartmouth was long distance. I was doomed. My sister Susanne was married and living in Ontario, my other sister was away so it was just me and my brother Eric out here. Eric made friends with the kids on the road almost immediately but it appeared there was no one out here my age. I was sitting on the front steps of the house in April when a girl about my age approached me and asked if I was the new girl in this house. I said yes and we exchanged names and she told me she lived down the road from me. She seemed really nice and for a while we did things together. She introduced me to other people in our area and told me what school I would go to and that we had to take a school bus, etc. There was nothing to do out here except walk along the highway or meet up at someone's house. Pretty boring. I actually looked forward to school starting.

September rolled around and I started school at the local Junior High School. It was the only Junior High in Sackville at the time. I was really excited about this new journey. Once I got settled into school, one of the boys started to talk to me. In no time at all, I had a crush on him. I didn't do anything about it but as we talked we discovered we didn't live too far from each other. I thought he was really nice and would blush when I saw him. Some girls I had met in my area soon discovered that I had a crush on this guy and everything changed for me again. They were a small but powerful clique and would stand together at the back of the classroom and make fun of me. The guy I thought was so nice actually "dropped me" and joined up with my tormentors. This betrayal hit me like a hammer blow. They would say things like "Did you really think someone would want to be with you"? "Hey Burns, I'm talking to you". "Hey Crispy Chicken". We all had to ride on the same school bus and the taunting would continue. One girl kept telling me she was going to beat me up. She frightened me but I tried to diffuse the tension by asking her in a nice voice "What did I do to you that you're treating me this way"? My question brought the direct opposite effect. The girl exploded in a fury of curses and threats. "We just decided that we don't like you. We don't want you here. You're too ugly. Why don't you move back to town, city girl? Oh, let me guess they wanted rid of you too cause nobody wants to look at you and your scars. You should have died. It would have been better for you." When I got off the school bus at my stop, they all got off. One girl hit me from behind. I had no idea how to fight as I was never involved in a fight before. As I stumbled forward she pushed me to the ground and my books went flying. She then attacked me with fists and feet. Blow after blow. Putting on a good show for the rest of her friends while they cheered her on and laughed at me. I tried to fight back but I didn't have a chance. When I got home my mother was upset at the condition of me and wanted to confront the girl's mother but I wouldn't let her. I told her it would just be worse for me and I went to my room and cried. I stayed in my room and played records all night long. Music was the way I soothed my pain. The next morning when I walked to the school bus they were all standing there and again the taunting started. At the bus stop, there was a little enclosed area that we could stand in to get out of the cold. They would not let me in and I had to stand by myself out in the elements. The taunting continued. It was more than I could endure. I turned and went back home. My father was still at home and he drove me to school that morning. When my tormentors discovered that I was in the school, they continued with the taunting. It practically became a ritual, a sick ritual as they followed me from class to class. I did not know that my father had spoken with the school principal and informed him of my situation and about my accident. He told them that I could not tolerate the cold and these students were deliberately standing in my way from getting inside and that we needed permission for me to be able to wear pants in the winter. At that time girls were not allowed to wear pants of any kind. The school board gave permission for me to wear them as long as it was dress pants, no jeans, shorts, etc... That opened up a new angle of attack for my tormentors. Now I was not only the burned, ugly girl, I was also the special girl. The girl who had favoritism on her side. No matter what I did they found a way to make it miserable for me. During this time I had to go to the hospital for a graft and release. This was kind of a relief for me to get away from them but I had no idea what was in store for me when I came back in bandages. When I did return to school, I had one area in bandages where the graft had been placed and a second area on my leg as the donor sight which was bandaged as well. The donor site was extremely painful and I would walk with a limp. When the attack came, it was the one girl. She came up behind me and kicked me right on the donor site. I screamed with the pain and collapsed to the floor. What they did next can only be described as a scene from a nightmare. While still on the floor, they gathered round and pretended to be trying to help me. "Oh you poor thing. What happened? Are you alright? Can we help?" I felt nauseated. My leg was bleeding through the bandage and the pain was horrific. A teacher came and helped me up. He took me to the Principal's Office. The principal asked me what happened and I told him. Someone kicked me in the leg but because they did it from behind I wasn't sure who did it. I told him they were not there to help me. They were smirking and giggling and pretending. They were the perpetrators. Then I noticed there was blood on my arm where they had put in the graft. The principal took me directly to my burn surgeon who advised that the graft was ok. It survived the attack and did not need further surgery. The donor site had a cut near the top and he tended to that. He medicated me and by this time my Dad had arrived at the doctor's and he and the principal had a good talk. This was bullying, at a criminal level. There was no doubt about it but there was nothing legal they could do about it. There were no laws with regards to bullying and I had to live with it. The girls, I later heard, were a little worried about the situation. They thought they might be in serious trouble. However, because nothing became of it, they soon started up again. The boy I had the crush on was still part of the group but he stayed in the back ground. One time I caught his eye and he started laughing at me, I lowered my eyes and turned away.

Gym class was always a nightmare because we had to wear gym suits. They were a one piece (top and bottom) with elastic on the bottom of the legs. They were very short and showed a lot of my scars. No one wanted to partner with me and I couldn't do much with no strength in my body. This always gave people the opportunity to snicker and make me feel foolish. Somehow I made it through my first year. But by now I was more scared of everyone and didn't know who to trust.

The summer was long and lonely for me as I stayed away from everyone. I had to for my own sanity.

In my second year of junior high, I set out to have a good year. The girls who had been my tormentors had moved on to something else. But a new problem was about to devastate me.

As I have said gym class was a nightmare for me and I hated gym days. In the locker room there was one bathroom stall and the rest was an open change area. Behind the wall was the shower. It was one large room with about 6 shower heads. It was mandatory that we shower after class. I would not shower in this open area, besides I didn't work up enough sweat to worry about it. Even I knew my body was horrible to look at and I wasn't going to put myself through that so I would change in the bathroom stall, safe behind the closed door. Or so I thought.

On this particular day everything was going OK. There were a couple of girls in my new class that were very loud and obnoxious and tended to pick on just about everyone. The area for our school housed black and white kids and sometimes there were clashes between the races. These girls were black and were letting the whites know that they were in charge. Most of the time they were just rude but you got used to it and didn't bother with it. Well this day we went to gym class. The boys and girls were separated by a divider in the gym. We could hear each other but could not see each other. Everything seemed to be going fine in the class up until they were climbing ropes. I had no strength to do it and I asked to be excused from it. One of the girls made such a fuss about it that I actually tried to do it. I tried as hard as I could but I couldn't do it. The gym teacher tried to explain my situation to the girls but they continued to argue with her. One girl just kept mouthing off and saying that I wanted special attention and pity. I told her I wanted no one's pity just a fair chance and this was something that I could not do. I did not have the strength or endurance to do it. Class finally ended and we headed to the locker room. Someone had already gone into the stall and I had to wait to change. The other girls were getting their showers and changing into regular clothes. When the stall door opened it was one of the girls from the group. I went in and started to change. Suddenly, one of the girls crawled under the door and into the stall with me. She threw open the door and gave me a terrific push out into the open area. It all happened very quickly. She was ranting about me being "special" and "Did I think I was too good to change with the rest of them?" I tried to explain that it was my burns that embarrassed me and made me feel very self-conscious. All this time, I was holding a towel over the front of my body. She whipped the towel from me leaving me exposed to everyone. The other girls in the room told them to back off and leave me alone but a mob mentality had taken hold of them. The lust to hurt and humiliate was gaining momentum. They grabbed my clothes and as they lifted them my bra fell to the floor. Now whereas I was burned all over my torso, my breasts were not developing because of the scar tissue. The muscle was burned away so the doctor had special pads made for my bra to indicate that I had breasts. This was done just to help me with my body image and to make me feel a little better about myself. One of the pads fell out. The ring leader picked it up and started to make fun of me. "Well, well, well, the girl wears falsies." She held it out for everyone and ridiculed me and humiliated me. I couldn't move or say anything. The mind is a wonderful thing. If you can make it shut down it can make the most unbearable things bearable. One of my class mates had made it past the girl and went to get the teacher. By the time the teacher came in I was completely shut down. The teacher sent the girls to the office and proceeded to help me get dressed. When the teacher took me to her office to talk about what happened, I could not speak. I could not put words together. The only sound I made was the sobbing that accompanied the flood of tears. I was in so much pain emotionally. She held me in her arms gently re-assuring me and encouraging me to let these emotions pass through me. She promised to help me all she could. As I gradually returned to my true self we spoke of the capacity for cruelty in some people. They are so evil that simply because I was different their animalistic impulse was to attack me. My father showed up and took me home. I stayed home for a while and was told the girls involved were expelled for what they did. An apology was supposed to be given but I refused it because it would not be a true apology. It would be just something they had to say to get back in school. Besides, I didn't want this to drag on.

There were some sneers by some of their gang when I returned to school but nothing I couldn't handle. It was mostly just snickering about my situation. It always struck me as odd that no one seemed interested in finding out from me how it happened. Life went on.

As horrible as these events were, I made myself focus on the fact that I had a few, very nice friends at school. One girl in particular, was a little spitfire and if someone said anything to her about me or anyone else for that matter she would hunt them down and challenge them to a fight. I smile today when I think about her. She was tiny but nothing was going to intimidate her. Trouble makers soon learned to keep their distance. As the school year went on I actually started to date boys from school or from the high school. I never got into any trouble. I didn't drink or do drugs but I did smoke like everyone else did at that time. In the language of those days, I was considered a "Goody, Goody". We would go to each other's houses on the weekends or go to the local dances which were held on Friday or Saturday nights. On Fridays it was held in the church hall and Saturdays it was at the Bedford Fire Station.

There was only one bus to our area and if you weren't on it, you weren't getting home. From the bus stop we had to walk another mile uphill at night. There were very few street lights and it was a little creepy. But it was worth it. My personality became that of a helper. I would help anyone in need of whatever. I still kept to myself a lot but boys started asking me out. I guess I was a nice person as I always seemed to have a boyfriend. I wasn't an easy target as I respected myself that way and I would definitely not allow anyone to see my body. My boyfriends were decent upstanding guys who liked me for me. I attended all the junior high and high school dances with my boyfriends. I found my niche, I loved to dance. At this time I was taking ballroom dancing lessons and if I say so myself, I was pretty good. I seemed to be able to follow any partner and passed the testing with ease. I loved the flow of the round waltz, the hype of the jive and the beat of the polka. I could dance to anything and I was very good on the teen dance floor. I honestly never sat out a dance unless I chose to. I never made it to my prom or my graduation ceremonies. I had been set up for a rather large surgery and the dates conflicted. I was disappointed but I had attended my boyfriend's proms in previous years so I knew what it was all about. When the summer arrived there were regular beach parties. If the party was through the day I would come up with an excuse not to be there. I was not getting into a swim suit so I missed out on a lot of fun. If it was an evening party, I would go. Most of them would go swimming but I would tell them I didn't like to swim at night and besides it was more fun on the beach. On two occasions I got thrown in the water with my clothes on. It was all in good fun. I also had the experience of going out with a new guy during one winter, when I would be all covered up. I really liked this boy and then winter passed and it got warmer. When he discovered I was burned more than he thought, he walked away. I hated the summers. Being burned has left its mark on me by what had happened to me so far. My self-esteem was not good about my future and I had a lot of self-loathing. I was convinced that I would be alone for the rest of my life. That no man would want to be with me. My body was just too horrific to look at. There was nothing sexy or attractive to entice a man and I couldn't bear the thought of showing my body to someone. But Springtime was a season I loved and looked forward to. There was one particular Spring that was shattered by an event that happened to me. It affirmed what I thought of myself at this time.

RAPED

It was a warm evening in June of 1968 and I was studying in my room for exams. I was cramming so much info into my head that I decided I needed to take a break. It was early so I would have plenty of time to come back to my studies. My Mom was in Windsor, Ontario visiting with my sister Susanne as she was having her first baby and Mom wanted to be there to help her. So again, it was Eric and I. Dad was downstairs and one of our neighbours came in. He and Dad started drinking and when I came downstairs to tell Dad that I was going for a walk to clear my head, he said OK. Just as I was going out the door, the neighbour asked me if I would take his dog for the walk with me as his wife was away and the dog hadn't been walked much. I said sure and asked him where the dog leash and dog were. He informed me that the backdoor was open, the leash was hanging on a hook and the dog should be right there in the kitchen.

I left the house and headed down the road toward his house to get the dog. There was not much distance between his house and ours, so I just strolled along. I got to the back door and found the leash. Just as I was about to put it on the dog, I was hit on the head from behind. My head was spinning and I had a hand over my mouth and was being dragged out the door and forced into a dump truck. I was confused and scared. As he threw me into his truck he told me not to try anything stupid or I may not make it back home. I was in complete panic and paralyzed with fear. And I was absolutely stunned as I realized at this point that this was the neighbour who was with my Dad! How did he get over here so fast and what was he doing? I was scared to death and asked him what he was doing and he told me to shut up. I was crying and holding my head where he hit me and begging him to let me go. He kept talking to me about horses and asked if I had seen this or that and sometimes I would respond and sometimes I didn't. I was really, really scared. He wouldn't stop the truck so I could jump out and when I tried he grabbed my arm really tight and kept hold of it for the rest of the ride. I was sobbing and told him he was hurting me but he wouldn't let go. I have no idea how he was shifting the truck while hanging on to me but somehow he managed to do it. He kept driving along the road, the road we lived on and came to an area that was desolate and woody. He stopped the truck and I begged him to let me out. He kept offering me cigarettes and I said no but to please let me go. At this point he leaned over and told me he had been watching me for a while and that my body was so maimed and ugly that no man was ever going to want to touch me and that he was going to show me what I would be missing. I begged him to let me go, please, please let me go. I now knew what his intentions were and screamed and screamed as he assaulted me. He was hurting me so much. He covered my mouth again to stifle my screams but it didn't matter anyway because there were no houses there for anyone to hear me. He stunk of whiskey and bad body odour. This assault continued for what seemed like a life time. He had ripped the pants I had been wearing but when he was done he told me to get dressed and that I wasn't to say anything to anyone about what just happened. I shook my head between my sobs and put my clothes on and sat on the seat. At this point he let go of me and went into his pocket to get his cigarettes. He dropped them on the floor of the truck and had to bend over to get them and with that I threw open the door and jumped out and started running. I knew where we were on the road and I knew we were not far from other neighbours and that I needed to get to one of them. I ran and ran and when I looked back he was running behind me and he had a crowbar in his hand. Oh my God he was going to kill me if he caught me and the fear was screaming in my body to run for my life. He was yelling that when he got hold of me I would never run again. I ran as fast as I could. I was asking God to help give me the strength to get away from him and get help. I knew I was bleeding in my private area but I needed help in the worst way. I made it to the neighbours and I banged and banged on the door afraid to look behind me in case he was there. When they answered it I said," Help me, please help me!" and I collapsed in their door. They took me inside and called the police and my father. I then told them what had just happened. The lady helped me clean up and Dad went home and got me some clean clothes. Then, together, my father and this neighbour went looking for the neighbour who had just raped me. I told Dad where the truck had been and when they got there they found it in the ditch. They then went to his house and his daughter said he was in bed and was asleep. My father, from what I was told, beat the man so badly that the other neighbour had to finally stop my father. When the police arrived, she claimed that her father had been home all night. She had been out earlier in the evening and had no idea what had happened. The Police had told her that was impossible because the truck was freshly ditched. She didn't want to believe what her father had just done and she didn't know the truck was missing. The police had me go to the hospital where I was examined. It was very intrusive considering what I had just been through and I required a few stitches. I sobbed through the examination and no one said a word. I could see the looks on the nurse's face and it was a look of pity but she said nothing.

I felt so dirty, I just wanted to shower and shower. They let me have a shower and gave me some medication. Dad took me home and I slept. The next morning the police came by and took my clothes to see if they could find anything on them. The neighbour had not been charged as yet because he claimed he was home all evening and that his truck was stolen. He was lying, but in the meantime, I had to try and pull myself together and carry on as if nothing had happened. Dad told me not to go to school the next day and called the school to get permission for me to write my exams when I returned. He told them what had happened which was probably a good thing. After I went back to school, the police showed up to have me go over my statement again.

It was a never ending nightmare that couldn't get worse. But it did.

Time went by and nothing was done about the rape. I couldn't understand why and when Mom returned from Windsor I told her what happened. She was shocked. She had been friends with the neighbour's wife and she went to see her about it. The wife told Mom that she had heard about it from her daughter and asked if I was alright. She didn't come to our house because she was too ashamed of what her husband had done and was afraid it would be to upsetting for me. But still nothing was done.

About six months later, the police came to the house again and returned my clothes. I asked why they were returning them, and wouldn't they need them for evidence. They told me that no charges had been laid and there was nothing they could do without my father pressing charges. I asked Dad why and he just said that he would talk about it later.

A year went by and one evening a knock came on the front door. I thought nothing of it and went to answer it. There, standing directly in front of me, just inches away, was the neighbor. I was horrified. I began to shake. I slammed the door shut and left him standing there. My father asked me who was at the door and I told him it was the rapist. He went to the door and to my shock and horror; he let him in the house. They sat there, together, and had a couple of drinks like nothing had happened. I couldn't believe it. I felt so betrayed, by my own father. My mother didn't know what to do either. She left the room and came upstairs with me. I was shaking and crying. I was so mad. I was trying to catch my breath. How could he do this to me, his own daughter? This was the beginning of my panic attacks. Every time that man showed up at our house, I would have trouble breathing. I never sought medical help for it as I did not know anything about panic attacks and just figured it was my way of handling the situation.

My Dad never did talk about it. He continued being friendly with this man and I continued to slam the door in his face and leave him standing there. Later, when I was much older, my father knew that I was pursuing the issue to see if there was anything that I could do now that I was an adult. He told me he didn't pursue it because we were neighbours. We were new to the area and he didn't want to start out on the wrong foot. One day, years later, my father came to my home and told me he had some news that I would probably be very happy to hear. He told me the neighbour was dying from cancer and apparently he was suffering quite badly with it. My reply was, "There is a God". I was angry at this news not because he had cancer but the fact that now I couldn't get justice for myself for what he did to me. I prayed to God to help me move on from the effects of the rape and to be able to trust people again. Two weeks later, my father announced that he died and I smiled. God answered my prayers. I very rarely told anyone about this because I really didn't have anyone to talk to. The girls around here were the ones who were giving me a hard time about my burns and I certainly didn't consider them friends that I would confide in, so I pretty well kept it to myself. The family that I ran to and helped me that night, moved from the neighbourhood so the secret was safe. But I never got over the betrayal from my father. The panic attacks continued. On January 7, 2013, I called the RCMP to see if there would be any record of this incident and I was informed that there was no record because charges were not filed, therefore no record and also if there had been charges it would have been sealed because I was a minor.

LIFE AS A TEENAGER

Now as hard as it is to believe there was a whole lot of other stuff going on at home during my school years. My father had an affair with a woman from our area and it appeared to be quite serious. Eric and I were the only ones in the house with Mom and Dad. Susanne lived in Ontario. We were in a country area and buses were few and far in between. We were more or less isolated and Dad was the only one who drove and he would not put himself out to drive anyone anywhere so we had to find our own way to places.

I went to the local junior high school and for me, I had to deal with the fact that this woman had her niece living with her and this niece went to my school. She would flaunt her new clothes and gifts that she got from her aunt's boyfriend, making sure that I knew about it. I would have friends come up to me and tell me what she was saying and I would just go to the washroom and cry. It was soon catching up with me and I was becoming depressed with it all and the school was noticing. The principal made an appointment with Mom and Dad to talk about my situation and I have no idea what was said but Dad abruptly made him leave and then started yelling at me. A few days later someone came to see Mom and Dad and unknown to me, they had arrangements for me to stay with another family. The family was my boyfriend's parents and they had agreed to keep me for whatever time I needed. I stayed with this family for about six months. Also at this time, the principal informed the woman that her niece would have to go to another school as she was out of area and I wasn't. The girl returned to her mother and that ended that phase. After all this, I returned home.

Before I left the house Eric and I were going crazy with Mom's delusions about Dad. Whenever we were with him we knew we had to face Mom when we got back. We didn't want to go with him because we knew what was going to happen but Dad wouldn't listen to us. He told us we were his children too and he could take us where he wanted. He wasn't the one who had to face the beatings when he left and they were brutal. It makes me cry when I think about the beatings that Eric took from her. He was too young and he couldn't defend himself and when I tried to help him it would get worse. She would drill him and hold him by the hair and hit and hit him because he wasn't giving her the answers she wanted or needed. So many times he was hit. I had it bad but Eric had it much, much worse because Dad would take him out a lot with him. Dad had to know what Mom was doing to Eric but still he would take him. I went with Dad once and I told the woman off and of course I had Dad's wrath to deal with and he never took me again but he would take Eric. My grandparents had moved to our area at this time and, of course, my grandmother embraced this woman and her kids. When any of Dad's siblings came here to visit, the woman was always invited for dinner and Dad would take Eric. He wanted Eric to be friends with her kids and Eric tried to keep this to himself but it eventually got back to Mom and we were brutalized in some way. When Eric or I would return from one of these outings, it got to the point where we would try to avoid her but there was nowhere to hide. None of the doors had locks except the bathroom and the closets had no doors. On a couple of occasions I would try to shelter Eric with my body and take the blows but she always managed to get to him. He was so scared of her, we all were. After a beating she would cry and tell us how sorry she was. It was Dad's fault. He was such a lousy bastard, a whore master, etc., and we had to listen to it. We tried to see it as an apology but it wasn't.

When I started dating and had a boyfriend with a car, Mom would pay the boy to go spy on my father. It was so humiliating and embarrassing to find this out and when I told Mom to please stop, she would just raise her fist at me and tell me to button it or lose it. I got to the point where I didn't bring anyone home and would meet up elsewhere so she couldn't get to them. This went on for about 3 years and then the woman gave my father an ultimatum. Either he leave Mom and be with her or she was going to move on. I believe that he was going to leave Mom until he found out through lawyers that Mom would be entitled to half of everything if he left. The thought of leaving Mom half the money, sent Dad into a tailspin. He was angry and indecisive and could not go through with the break. Running out of patience, the woman ended the relationship with him. I know they stayed in touch because she eventually married a friend of my father's and the three of them would get together occasionally.

And so we finally had a family for a couple of years. We thought this was all behind us but it wasn't. At least we were now too big for beatings but we still got the "knuckle".

GETTING MARRIED

I started dating my future husband when I was 16. He was 6 years older than me but his maturity level was probably around 19 at that time. He worked shift work
for the local air line and I was still in school. On his days off he would come by the school and pick me up so I didn't have to take the bus. I was pretty excited that an older man was paying attention to me and seemed to really like me. There were some age difference issues but they usually got worked out. We spent a lot of time driving around or hanging out at my place. When I was close to my 18th birthday, he proposed to me and I was flabbergasted. This guy actually wanted to be with me. He knew I was burned and to what severity and still he wanted to be with me. I would say I wasn't a bad looking girl. I was thin and had long brown hair but certainly no beauty queen. I always tried to keep myself nice with clothes because I knew there wasn't anything nice under them. It's a practise I still do today. So he went to my parents and asked their permission to marry me and my father said no. He felt I was too young and he was immature and that our ages were too far apart. I know my mother tried to convince him otherwise because she felt there was not going to be much opportunity for me and perhaps we should take it. But Dad stuck to his guns and said no.

I wasn't going to have my dreams shattered by my father again and so we applied to the court for a marriage license and because I was under 19, I still needed a parent signature. I took the papers to my mother and begged her to sign them. She was already practically in favour of the marriage and when I said this may be my only chance to get married, she signed them. We took the papers back and filed them and then we booked the courthouse for a wedding. We eloped. I wore a simple yellow and white dress that I borrowed from my sister. I was married the day before my 18th birthday. We had already picked out an apartment and we had a little gathering that evening. My father would not come. The next time I spoke to my father he didn't congratulate us. He turned to me and said, "Little girl by the time you are 25 you will be a fully mature adult. Unfortunately, he will remain as immature as he is today, and this will destroy your marriage…mark my words." I walked away in a huff. We settled into married life.

We were both working and life was good. About a year later, I discovered I was pregnant but within a couple of months I miscarried. This pattern continued on for the next couple of years. I had miscarried 4 times. I went from doctor to doctor wanting to know why I couldn't get past 3 months. They ran every test possible on both of us and the final conclusion was that my insides were probably damaged from the burn injury and I wouldn't have any kids. I was devastated. When I told my husband the news he really didn't seem too upset by it which confused me at the time. I thought he wanted a family as much as I did. I got pregnant again and this time the doctor made me stop work, put me on bed rest and monitored me closely. I was in danger of miscarrying again but this time I carried the pregnancy through. When I was pregnant my skin could not stretch enough. As I got bigger my skin actually began to tear open at the hips. The doctors wanted to do skin grafting but I said no because I didn't want the baby to be under anesthesia. Nothing was going to harm this baby. I was going to protect it with everything I've got. Instead of grafting, I chose bandages, abdomen pads and a little more pain. About this time

I noticed that hubby was working a lot but thought nothing of it. I figured with the baby coming he was working to make extra money. I found out after the baby was born that he was seeing my best friend. I was emotionally drained at this point. I couldn't believe it. I told her to stay away from my house. Eventually things settled down between my husband and I and we decided to give it another go. When our first child was 18 months old I gave birth to my second child, only this time tension between us was very thick.

I noticed little things. He was again working a lot, or so I thought and he was now making references to my burns when he would introduce me to people. I thought it was strange but didn't pay a whole lot of attention to it. But it became more and more. He would say things like "This is my wife Debbie, she is a burn victim, but it doesn't bother me". What was he doing? Was he trying to portray himself as some kind of hero because I'm burnt and it didn't "bother" him?Had I become a burden to him? I was still having a lot of surgeries but he knew what he was getting into before we married. In fact, I had explained thoroughly and repeatedly what the future held for me. These remarks continued and then one day I got a phone call from one of his co-workers who told me he thought I should know that he wasn't working all the time. He was seeing the woman he was with before. My best friend. I confronted him with the phone call and he never denied it. I found it a bit strange that he was seeing her again because I knew she had married. We separated, and by the time I was 25, I was divorced. My father's words came back like a smack in the face. We stayed friendly for the sake of the kids. I never regretted marrying him. We did love each other at first but it wasn't strong enough to overcome our mistakes. Life went on, he paid his child support, I went back to work and the kids seemed happy enough. We are still very friendly to this day.

ROUND 2 - HERE WE GO AGAIN

I met my second husband through my brother. There was an instant attraction and we discovered we had a lot in common. We had a lot of fun together and he accepted my children as part of the package and they liked him. As time went on he moved in with me. Shortly after that he had applied for a new job. This job would be a lot more money and would benefit our household greatly. There was only one downside to this. The job was with The Department of Fisheries and Oceans and he would be out to sea for most of the time. He asked me to marry him. He told me I was his soul mate and he dedicated the song "You're in my heart" by Rod Stewart to me. I loved him very, very much and I missed him terribly when he was gone. We had so many good laughs when he was home but he was home for so little time. When we decided to plan our wedding, we did it by mail and I had to get all the arrangements done. We had decided that whereas I had eloped for my first marriage and that this was his first marriage that we were going to have a big wedding. My dress was a real wedding gown but instead of white, I chose pink with a hat instead of a veil. The dress itself was white with pink lace overlay. It was beautiful. I made all the preparations and he arrived home just 2 days before the wedding. It was a beautiful winter wedding and we celebrated it with all our friends and family. There were about 200 guests and we had a wonderful evening. We couldn't go anywhere for a honeymoon so we went to a couple of different hotels over a week just spending the time together and touring our home town. It was very relaxing for both of us but finally it was time to go home. He spent a couple of days with the kids because he was sailing in the next few days and it was coming up fast. And so the day arrived that he had to leave and I cried. I saw him off and went home to an empty apartment. That evening my father came by. I began having pains in my chest and I was having trouble breathing. I thought I was having a heart attack. He called an ambulance and I was taken to the hospital where it was discovered I had a collapsed lung. Everyone was making jokes to me about landing in hospital right after the honeymoon. It was good laughter and what I needed at the time. We got a message to my husband and told him not to worry. I would be fine. It was while I was in hospital that I realized I had missed my period. I figured it was all the excitement with the wedding and all because I had my period the previous month but I was now overdue. I told the doctor in the hospital because they were X-raying me every day to see how the lung was progressing. They immediately did a pregnancy test and the doctor announced the results by saying, "Surprise you're pregnant." I was thrilled. They told me I was not very far into it and they were stopping the x-rays immediately. I was having his baby and I was delighted. When he telephoned me from the first port he got into, I was back home. I told him he was going to be a Dad and he was thrilled. Again, the only down side was that he was going to be gone for most of the pregnancy. It was a good thing we had good friends who came by all the time to see if I needed anything. When he got home I was quite filled out and he was beaming from ear to ear. I could see it on his face as they docked the ship and when the walkway was put out he came a running. We couldn't have been happier.

He was only home for a few days and had to go again. The next time he came home, he was on leave because the baby was due soon. Our little bundle of joy came into this world exactly 9 months and 2 days after our wedding. He was definitely conceived on our honeymoon. During the pregnancy I started having negative thoughts about my husband being away all the time. I started to think that he really didn't want to be with me. I asked him to leave the ships, that I was lonely and I needed him here and the kids needed him. He refused because the money was good. I took this to mean he didn't want to be around me. I was blaming the burns for my misfortune and couldn't put my head around it. He tried to prove to me that he was devoted to me and adopted my first two children. We had talked about that before we were married and were going to approach my ex-husband about it but we had not been married 2 weeks when I got a phone call from my ex- husband's lawyer asking if my new husband was interested in adopting the kids. My ex didn't want to pay child support anymore. Nothing made sense to me; it had to be the burns. He again sailed and I had decided to go back to work. My mother agreed to look after the kids, so I got a job.

Everything seemed OK at first but with him being away so much I started to go out with co-workers. Gradually I began writing fewer and fewer letters.I was lonely, young and wanted attention but my husband wasn't here to give it to me. When he returned home from one of his trips, I again asked him to leave the ships and again the answer was no. So I told him we needed to separate because I was lonely. Reluctantly he finally gave in. He told me this was not what he wanted but I, on the other hand, had changed.

He sailed again and came home early because my father had called him and advised him that I was seeing someone and that he should come home. He was right.I was involved with a co-worker who was the total opposite of my husband. My husband was a good husband, father and provider.This man I was infatuated with had none of these qualities. In fact, he was a disaster as a human being. I couldn't decide what to do. I didn't love this guy but I was totally infatuated with him. I loved my husband. I tried several times to leave this guy but I kept going back and all the while my husband was waiting for me. He tried to help me in every way that he could, but I kept going back to this guy.

THE ABUSER

The only way I can write this section is to go right into it from my marriage. I know it doesn't make any sense that I loved my husband and at the same time I had a powerful emotional attraction to this guy. As I said, my husband was so good and decent and this guy was the total opposite... My husband had the odd drink, didn't do drugs, was kind and gentle and this guy did all of it. My husband had a good paying job and this man was a truck driver at the same place that I worked. He was good to me in the beginning but as time went on things changed. It started with a shove one evening after he had been drinking. Then it went to him cornering me and a slap. It accelerated from there. If I was to so much as talk with my husband or any other man then he assumed I was sleeping with him and I would get beat up. One time he broke my left arm and I went to the Emergency Department. The doctor who looked after me knew it was domestic violence and told me he could help. I told him I didn't know what he was talking about, that I was playing baseball and I got in the way of the bat. The bruises were getting hard to hide and more than once I had a black eye. I would go to work and make excuses for what had happened to me but I knew that they knew. One of my bosses actually tried to help me by keeping him on the road all the time. The beatings finally overcame the infatuation and I moved out. It was Christmas Day. I had arranged with my husband to take the kids after they opened their presents and to keep them over night so I could get the move done. I gave him the new address and he hugged me and wished me a Merry Christmas. The guys at work had actually given up their day to move me. It was set for 10 in the morning by them because they claimed they usually had nothing to do until supper time and they came and loaded everything into the truck. We threw everything into boxes and loaded up. We moved quickly because he was due home that evening or the next morning and I needed to be gone. The last thing on the truck was my Christmas tree fully decorated. It was quite a sight. The guys said, "last on first off". We arrived at my new home and I thanked them. They all hugged me and wished me well. I proceeded to put my new home together and by the time my husband brought the kids home the next evening, I had everything done and put away and we celebrated together. I cooked a dinner the next day for all of us and we were a family again.

Things went as expected when the guy came home and found an empty apartment. I left what was required of me by law but this was not going to be the end of it. He was not going to go away easily. I was communicating with my husband and it looked like we might be healing from all this. He was there for me so often I don't know why I couldn't break the ties with the other one. I did everything that we planned. I didn't give him my phone number and I wouldn't tell him where I lived and I even changed jobs to keep him away from me but he would always show up in the most unexpected places. One day he got a friend to follow me home and found out where I was living. He kept showing up at the door and after a while he broke me down and I let him back in. He made all the usual promises that it would never happen again and he was so sorry and I bought it hook, line and sinker. I was sucked in again and this time when the abuse started it was far worse than anything I went through before. When I told him to leave he threatened to hurt my kids and I was afraid that he would actually do it.

My kids hated him. They saw what was happening to me and were helpless to help me. My panic attacks were increasing in number and severity.

One evening we were camping and my whole family was there. He was very sweet to my family and they didn't know a lot about what was happening to me. Being an abuser, he kept us separated a lot from my family and so they were only hearing bits and pieces. When they asked me, of course I told them nothing.

That evening, he had been drinking and was doing some drugs. I learned quite quickly that when he was drunk, that brought on one kind of abuse. When he did drugs, there was another kind of abuse. But, when he did both together he was deadly. On this particular evening I don't even remember what set him off. It was probably me telling him to slow down and that would be enough to send him into a rage. He came at me in the trailer. He was choking me and my kids were trying to get help. My sister came in and tried to get him off me and he hit her. He left the trailer and the camp and we had no idea where he went. We decided that we were going home as it was probably a safer place to be. I called the police and had them meet me at the house. I showed them the marks on my neck and on my face and legs and that I wanted to report the assault. The drunken attack was so vicious that I believed he had actually tried to kill me. As the police were taking my statement, he walked into the house. They asked him if he had done this to me and he said, "Hell yes". They immediately put him in hand cuffs. All the while he was shouting obscenities, threats and insults at me. "I'll take that crispy fried body and burn it up more". The cops yanked him out and took him away. The police said that since he admitted to the assault I didn't have to worry anymore and they would get a restraining order to keep him away. The kids were in their rooms and I went to them and told them it was over and we all piled in my bed and had a good sleep. But it still wasn't over. One day I was alone in the house, the kids had gone out with my husband. While straightening the curtains in the living room window, I happened to look out and saw him walking on the road heading towards the house. In a panic, I called the police and told them he was here. They couldn't believe it. They had just released him and told him to stay away from here and here he was. He came to the door and I wouldn't let him in. When the police arrived, he told them that he had to come back because he needed clothes and his gear as he was heading out west. It was all strictly business and on the up and up... he said. They let him in, he got his stuff and left. He fired up his rig and drove away. I thought that would be the end of it.

My husband and I decided to start fresh. We talked about all that had happened and I told him that no matter what, it was him that I loved and he told me he would always love me and stand by me. I couldn't believe my ears. After all I had put him through he still loved me. He told me ours was a love that only happens once and no matter what path we took that love would always be there between us. He was so right.

We decided that now was the time for us to get our own home and start over. We were excited about this new venture and started looking at homes. When we found one that we liked we had my Dad go and look it over and get his opinion.

My husband didn't have any parents here. He was estranged from his father and his mother had passed away so we relied on my father's opinion. We finally decided on a split level in our home town. The basement was not finished and we needed a couple more bedrooms so my Dad and my husband went right to work to build it. We ended up with a four bedroom home that I loved. We were doing great and the kids were settled and life seemed good except for one thing. My husband was still away a lot. In one year I had seen him for a total of 10 days out of that year. Again I began wondering why he didn't want to give up the job and be home with me. I told him I felt like a whore in port. He would get home, we would be together and the next day he was gone. Not a good life but I knew what I had gone back into. I continued to work and all seemed fine and then one day, I was at the bank. When I went back to my car, I was about to get in when I sensed someone was behind me, I turned and it was him. He was back and he had a vengeance to settle with me. I told him to leave me alone I was not interested anymore and he laughed at me. I tried to get into my car but he blocked me. I told him I needed to get back to work, again he laughed. Luckily for me another person we both knew came up and started talking to him and I was able to get in the car, lock it and drive away. I got back to the office and to my shock and horror, he showed up there. I told him to leave but again he laughed and informed me that he had just been hired as a new driver. I could have cried. I went into a panic attack.

He knew that my husband was away and he had looked in my personal file at work to get my phone number. He started calling my house almost immediately and I just kept hanging up. Eventually he started showing up at my door. I told my husband what was going on and he couldn't believe it. I knew he was worried and he had every right to be. I tried very hard not to be taken in by this guy again. One night when the kids were all out for an overnight with friends he showed up. I again became involved with him. Our love/hate relationship was back. My husband moved out of our home and told me to decide once and for all. He couldn't keep living like this. I thought I was going to lose my mind. How could I keep doing this to myself? I knew what this guy was all about. He was no good for me but I kept going back for more. It took a while for me to get him out of my system and the final straw was after a beating I took from him. When I went to work the next day my boss saw the black eye. There was no way to hide it and he asked me if I could stay a little late after work as he had something he needed to get done. He saw the panic in my face and told me not to worry he would let the guy know that I was required to work. After closing I asked him what work he had for me. He responded by saying "Let's just go down the road and grab a bite to eat and then we'll get to it." I said OK and we went to the little restaurant close to where we worked. He was an excellent boss and I always felt comfortable in his company. After dinner we headed back to the office, or so I thought. He took a turn off and I immediately started to panic. He told me not to be frightened; he was only trying to help me. He turned into a drive way and led me into a building. I had no idea where I was. A lady came out and spoke with him. It was obvious they knew each other. He told me her name and she told me to come with her. I looked at him and he told me it was OK and that he would be back for me in an hour or so. The lady took me into an office and told me my boss was concerned for me and that he had brought me to an Al-Anon meeting. Al-Anon is for the victims of alcohol abuse. My boss felt I needed their help. I sat in her office and I cried and cried. She quietly let me shed all the tears I had inside me. When I recovered my composure she took me into another room with other people who had been abused as well. They all told their stories and when it came to me I told them it was too soon for me to talk about it. It was too fresh and I again started crying. I felt comforted from what I had heard that night and continued attending the meetings. I learned that I was what they referred to as an "enabler". I was enabling him to drink because I was the one calling in sick for him and making excuses for him. He knew I was weak and he was using it against me. I told him I wanted him to leave my home and he laughed at me. I had to physically go and get him a room in a rooming house and move his belongings there while he was away. I called my doctor and I told him I thought I was having a nervous breakdown, that I needed to go to a mental hospital and I couldn't take anymore.

My doctor said, "Whoa there Debbie, you are not the type to go to a mental hospital," and he sent me to see a psychiatrist. The psychiatrist told me about a 6 week program that was starting up on " Stress Management" and suggested I go to it. It was about abuse, enablers, co-dependency,ways to handle stress, etc. It was at this point that I went to my boss and gave notice that I was leaving.I had to take care of myself for a change. He was a fine man and wished me well.He waved good bye and said "Debbie, if you ever need a job, just call me."I continued going to the Al-Anon meetings until the Stress Management program started.Then I settled into the new program.

THE BREAKDOWN

Thank God the psychiatrist recommended the Stress Management Program.

My entering that program was the best thing I could have done for myself. I hesitated at first because there is a lot of stigma around mental issues but I have to say for me it was the best thing. The program was attended by about 10 people. Each one had their own reasons for being there. I found out that I was the only one in the group who had not tried to commit suicide. That information stunned me. One of the participants was a lady who was about my age and we hit it off right away. We partnered up on everything and had a great time. Once, during an exercise class, the teacher was playing music. My new friend and I started jive dancing while all the rest of the group where running around the gym. The teacher was enjoying our "show" and told the rest of the group that the reason she didn't stop us was because we were doing more exercise than the rest of them. We just thought we were being smart alecks. A friendship developed and has grown over the years. We are there for each other no matter what it is. Many days can go by without talking to each other and when one of us calls it's as though we just spoke yesterday. It is a friendship built on trust for each other. We talk about everything.

Part of this program was to meet with a psychiatrist and therapist to discuss the problems that had brought us to the program. After explaining everything that I had been through the doctor told me that my main problem was that I had no self- esteem. My whole life has consisted of other people making decisions for me and when I became of age they continued in that role. This co-dependency situation was especially powerful between me and my father. The psychiatrist also stated that because my being raped had not been taken care of by my father, I was totally broken by his betrayal. I had learned to trust no one and because of all the bullying and remarks about my burn injury, I felt unworthy of love. It was actually me putting myself into these situations. I didn't feel that I deserved love and I didn't know how to respond to love. My inability to make good, positive decisions for myself was just me figuring that was all I deserved. With respect to my burns, he really couldn't respond. He had no idea what it was like to be a victim of such a horrific accident and to survive it. He was quite willing to listen but that was about all he could do. He explained to me that the panic attacks were being caused from all the dysfunction in my life and that this was my body reacting to the stress. That could be controlled and if I was lucky could eventually go away.

Through all this I continued to talk with my husband. He was still there for me.

My husband and I resumed living together in the house and although we tried, it wasn't working out. There was no doubt that we still loved each other but there was just too much water under the bridge and too much uneasiness between us.

We both agreed that we needed to move on with our lives. It was especially true for him. He had been waiting for me for a long time and now he needed a life.

We separated and we both began to date. For both of us there was nothing serious at first and then we both settled into common law situations. We still hadn't divorced and were both comfortable with that. Then my new partner asked me to marry him.

ROUND THREE

Earl and I had been living together for a couple of years and we had our ups and downs. We both had kids from previous marriages and it was a little hard getting them to accept us. My son was very much a protector of me and his son definitely wanted Earl back with his mother so it was a little difficult at times. We both decided that we did not want any more children. That was not an issue with me because I couldn't have any more children anyway. I had gone back to work and we were living in my home. Neither one of us were divorced and we were comfortable with that as were our spouses. It left us all with a safety net I guess. My husband had met up with a woman and they moved in together. We all talked politely with each other. We weren't "buddy buddy" but we were sociable when we were together. My husband really wanted to take his time and know more about this woman. She also had a child. My partner's wife had also allowed a man to move in, but things changed in his situation. She became very nasty and unfriendly. We used to go to her house on holidays and birthdays to see what the kids got but once she got with him that was no longer permitted.

Over time, I began to meet up with my husband for coffee at the local coffee shop or at his place. Naturally, she began to resent it. What no one knew was that on my birthday or his we would call each other and when we got computers we would email each other on our anniversary. We also said happy anniversary and would talk about how much we still loved each other.

But we were with other partners now and we had to carry on. We made new friends and did different things.

About this time my oldest daughter was acting up and was with a guy I really didn't like. The next thing I knew on her 16th birthday she moved out against my will and a few months later she was pregnant.

I convinced her to move back home and when the baby was born she stayed with us for a while. Earl had a mobile home that he rented out and I convinced him to let her and the baby live there. Unfortunately, that didn't work out too well. The father of the baby was still partying and my daughter wanted to do the same. One night Earl and I were attending a banquet and I asked my daughter to look after my son for the night. He was around 10 years old at the time. When we returned home from the banquet, I received a phone call from a neighbour of my daughter's that the baby had been crying for hours and that someone called social services on her. I found out from my son that he was left alone with the baby and he couldn't get the baby to stop crying. Just as I was going out the door to go to him, the phone rang again and it was a social worker. I told her I was on my way to get the baby. She said she would call me in the morning. I got to the mobile home and gathered up the baby and as many clothes as I could and took the kids home. I got the baby settled and my son to bed and feel asleep exhausted only to have the Dad call me at 3 a.m. wanting to know where the baby was. I told him I had her and I was keeping her. Now I had to tell you all this because this played an important role between me and Earl. If you remember, we didn't want any more kids and when I announced that I was keeping the baby, he was not happy about it. He more or less told me it was him or the baby. One or the other had to go. I didn't even bat an eye when I gave him my answer. He could look after himself, she couldn't and if I didn't keep her she would end up in the social services system and I wasn't having that. He had some thinking to do. Was he staying or was he leaving my home? We talked a lot about the situation and he finally relented. He saw my point of view and said he would stay. We settled in to our new routine having a baby in the house and the kids finally settled in together. Time went on and the kids grew up. My son and Earl's son became best of friends, brothers, and are there for each other through thick and thin. When Earl's son was getting married, my son was best man and it made us both proud. The girls never got close. There was a lot of jealousy from Earl's daughter towards the baby and that never changed to this day. Life with Earl certainly was different. I knew that he loved me and I loved him as well, it was just a different love from what I had with my second husband.

Earl is very much a handy man, so was my father, and he had a temper, so did my father. This temper of his was only verbal, never physical, but it was a controlling temper and I knew we were in trouble because I was not ever going to let a man control me again. After one particular fight I told him to leave, I was not his personal property and I sure as hell was not taking orders. If he wanted that then he needed to go back home to his mother. She would take it from him because that's how his father treated his mother. This was a very angry fight, but we were not "at war" and did not fight all the time. Actually we had many long and deep conversations about our relationship and our behaviors. He was a good man but I was convinced his bad behaviors were learned behaviors and could be changed. I pointed this out to him and he started to recognize when he was doing it and sometimes I had to give him our code word to make him stop. Now this all makes him sound like a horrible person but he's really not. He is very supportive of me and what I need to do for me and there is no question that he loves me. He admits that he is lost without me and never wants to think about not being with me. I feel the same way. When I had surgeries for my burns he was always there for me. He would help with dressing changes and anything I needed. I could see the pity in his eyes sometimes when these operations came up but he always put on a good face and did whatever was needed to be done. He became my support person for these occasions and he would listen to me when I cried and sometimes he would cry with me but we got through it together. It was his love and guidance that led me to take the most important step in my recovery. I would have walked away from that opportunity and let my fears dominate my life. But because of his support, I am where I am today. He has seen me through the changes I made in myself and encouraged me in every avenue of this journey. This is my journey but he is very much a part of it. Because of him I am grounded, I have grown and I am happy.

INTRODUCTION TO
BURN SUPPORT

After one of my operations, I received a phone call from an individual who identified herself as "the Burn Unit Manager". She asked me if I would be interested in attending a Burn Camp for adults and children. The Nova Scotia Fire Fighters Burn Treatment Society was organizing it and seeking participants. I asked her to send me additional information and I would let her know. I was hesitant as I was now 40 years post burn and never had contact with another burn survivor other than once in the hospital as a child. I had met 2 sisters who were burned on Halloween but had lost contact with them after a couple of years. I had seen another gentleman once in the hospital as a young adult but we never said anything other than a mute hello as we passed in the hospital hallways. . We were both too scared to say anything.Later on in life we would meet up again and have a good laugh about that.I received the package of information and filled out the paperwork. Upon inquiring, I was informed that I could bring my partner with me so that made it a little easier to decide. He was my rock and I knew I could do it with him, so I sent in the paperwork and waited for the details.The camp was organized at a local attraction theme park and was to last for 5 days.I recall being very nervous when we arrived. While signing in I noticed that there were lots of kids and then I spotted some other adults. Some adults were easy to notice as they had facial burns.Others, like myself, were not so obvious. I also noticed that even though we were in the middle of a summer heat wave, we were all dressed in long sleeves and pants. Only the kids were in shorts and they were all running around and making themselves known. The gentleman, Buzz, who was in charge of the Burn Support Group, introduced himself, then asked me to join him and the others in another room. I went to the room with him and sat down, said hello to everyone and shut up. I immediately grabbed

Earl's arm and held on to it. This was the first time I had ever engaged with another adult burn victim and I was uncomfort-able. Once we were all there, he had us introduce ourselves to each other and state a little about ourselves and our accident, if we choose to do so. It was not mandatory for us to share our information if we were uncomfortable with it. I stated my name and how I was burned and how long ago. The only grace for me was I spotted the gentleman that I had seen in the hospital some years ago and he also acknowledged me. When we finally took a break I told Earl I wanted to go home. I wanted to get out of there. This was not a place for me. He tried to talk me out of it and I think he signaled Buzz somehow and told him I wanted to leave. Buzz asked me to please consider staying. But I was determined I was leaving. As we walked back to the car my partner was still talking to me, telling me to at least try, stay for the day and if I felt the same way the next day, then we would leave. I sat in the car, lit up a cigarette and began sobbing. I didn't really understand why I was crying and why I was so scared but the fear was there and the panic was real. I struggled with these feelings because somewhere deep in my mind I believed that this was very important. That it was something I must do. Although I was still ambivalent and afraid, I calmed down, got out of the car and walked back to the meeting. Buzz was pleased I returned and we proceeded with the day. We, the adults, were staying in a local motel. That night after the evening meal and events we returned to our room. I dropped from exhaustion but it was a good exhaustion. I rested there, on the bed for a while. Because it was such a nice evening my partner suggested we go outside. The next thing I knew there were a lot of us sitting out.

Our conversations started out as just small talk. But soon the casual talk ended and we got more into our stories. We talked and talked and talked until way past midnight. It was quite late when we said our good nights, but it was certainly the opener we needed and we were all looking forward to the next day. I was no longer uncertain. The decision for me had been made. I was staying.

Each day was filled with a different agenda but there were always the talk sessions. These talk sessions quickly became the most important part of the day. We were looking forward to them. We discovered that most of us had dealt with the same issues. Burn awareness and support groups had not yet been organized. This was all new and we were glad to see that something was being done about this hidden cause. It was decided at that time to start up the burn support group and we have continued with this. By the end of the week, it was interesting to note that we were all in shorts and sleeveless shirts. It was an emotional journey and a healing journey for most of us and we hated to see it end. We had made a number of new friends and looked forward to getting together again the following year. Burn camp had become official. I became a member of the Burn Support Group. At one of the meetings I learned that our main functions were advocacy, education and support. I also learned of a conference that was held every year in the United States called the "World Burn Conference". It was sponsored through an organization called the "Phoenix Society". Buzz explained that it was for burn survivors all across North America and that our group was invited to send some people. During the time this was under discussion I was absent due to a surgery I required. When I returned a delegation had already been selected and the matter was settled. I was disappointed because I was interested in attending. Buzz then told me about another group who sponsored people to go to these events. I contacted them, described my situation and they offered to sponsor me. I was ecstatic. The conference was held in Grand Rapids, Michigan and it was more than I could ever have dreamed of. It was so over whelming and emotional. At one point Buzz saw me with a confused look on my face and asked me what was wrong. I asked him, "Buzz, what am I doing here"? He laughed and said "Are you not a burn survivor?" "Yes", I said "But compared to the rest of the people here I look like I was only singed." I was lucky that I could cover my burns.Some people were not that fortunate and I understood. I did belong there and I was taking in everything I could. I didn't make a formal presentation or make a speech but I listened to every word and I talked to as many people as I could.

Over the years I continued with the support groups and each year I was sponsored by either The Nova Scotia Fire Fighters Burn Treatment Society, Canadian Burn Foundation or my own private sponsors but I managed to get to these conferences and each year I got stronger and more self-assured with regards to my burns. Our leader, Buzz, became ill and passed away. He was a friend, a mentor, a motivator and an organizer. I missed him terribly. Our group was weakened by his passing but he had organized a strong group. He was replaced by a woman who was very comfortable with her injury. She showed by example that the burns weren't going to stop her, and they didn't need to stop any of us from reaching our goals or living our lives. Our group continued under her Presidency for five years. At the end of her tenure, I was elected President. It is a position I still hold to this day.

I attended the World Burn Conferences (WBC) over the years and each year it grew larger and larger. In fact WBC was getting too big and it was losing the advantages that came with a smaller, more personal approach. Because of this the Canadians in attendance decided to organize our own conference. We had our first conference in Winnipeg, Manitoba, June 2005. Everyone who attended from here told what a wonderful experience they had.Unfortunately for me, I missed attending due to my granddaughter having her tonsils removed. It was very intimate and personal and they loved it better than the WBC. At the Winnipeg conference, another meeting was held among the Canadians and the Nova Scotia Firefighters Burn Treatment Society, Halifax, Nova Scotia decided to host the next conference and we were truly excited. Everyone helped where we could and the Halifax conference, 2006, was also a success. The next year, 2007, the WBC conference was held in Vancouver, BC. Another meeting was held with the Canadians to decide if we wanted to continue with the Canadian Conferences. It was decided to form our own group. Several people signed up to be part of this group and a board was formed. Since we were dispersed across Canada, we organized by telephone and email. Our first order of business was to decide on a name and logo for our group. We decided on The Canadian Burn Survivor Community and the logo was designed by my son, Andrew. We were off and running. As a point of clarification, the WBC conferences are held every year in different states and sometimes in Canada. The Canadian Conference is held every 2 years in different provinces. So every even year there is a Canadian Conference.

TODAY

Today, I am still President of the Nova Scotia Burn Support Group and I am also the Secretary/Treasurer for the Canadian Burn Survivor Community. I am also the mother of 3 wonderful children, 2 step children, foster mom of 3 boys at the present and grandmother to 8 beautiful children. It has been a very rewarding experience to have overcome my dysfunctional home as a child, my dysfunctional life as an adult, to now. I survived this dysfunction from my childhood and I survived the rape and I survived the abuse and I survived the divorces and I grew as a person. My survival was to be put to the test again when I suffered a heart attack on June 13, 2011. This was caused by a couple of factors. My life of emotional stress and physical operations weakened my heart and I was also a smoker. To add to my stress, my ex-husband, who was my soul mate, was getting married. I struggled with this upcoming marriage. On the weekend of the wedding I thought I was losing my mind. I couldn't function. My family figured out what it was but I didn't. On Monday morning I took a heavy feeling in my chest and pain ran down my left arm and I knew I was in trouble. I called an ambulance and was rushed to the hospital; I was having a heart attack. I cried and cried as I lay on that bed knowing that I could die and no one knew I was there and all I could think about was that he had gotten married and I had lost my best friend. It was the end of the relationship that had lasted for over 25 years. It was like a death to me. When Earl came in and saw me there he was shocked but he said he knew why I was there and that we would talk later. Now was not a good time. I had 3 stents put in and after a week in the hospital I was sent home with my list of instructions and I carried on. When everyone was either at work or in school and I was alone I continued to cry for the loss I felt. I felt guilty to all those around me that loved me and were trying to help and protect me. I realized that I needed to talk to someone and so I made an appointment to talk with a psychologist that I knew for a while.

I told him my situation and he told me that what I had told him made sense. It may not make sense to others but for me it was like a death and they needed to respect my grieving. I realize that it was so difficult for me to accept this marriage because he had gone through so much with me emotionally. The psychologist told me I now needed to talk with Earl and explain things to him. I told him he was hurt and I knew it, but it had nothing to do with what I felt for him and I needed to reassure him that I was still with him 100 per cent and hope he could understand.

Also at this time I have been diagnosed with diabetes. This is an uphill battle. Combined with the diet for heart attack, trying to quit smoking and the diet for diabetes it is very hard but I will do it.

What I have learned over the years is that I am a very caring person. I love being in the care giving role and helping new burn survivors overcome some of their hurdles. I visit them in the hospital and keep in touch once they are released. Our Burn Support Group is still holding regular meetings. I also go into schools and speak on a burn awareness and prevention programs. I do this on a volunteer basis but hope for a donation to our support group.

The Canadian Burn Support Community has now held two conferences under this name and both have been a success. It is meaningful to me to be involved as a member of the Board for such a wonderful group of people and my heart and passion belongs to the burn community.

I have spoken at the Canadian Association of Burn Nurses and have been on different panels at the World Burn Conference as well as the Canadian Burn Conferences.

What I have learned from my past is that your past can control your future if you let it. Or you can move away from it. It took years for me to see this and I have to admit most of my awareness came from the burn support group. I had no idea that I was carrying around baggage from my accident and all the years of torment until I started attending the World Burn Conferences and hearing other people speak. They stirred up deep memories and feelings inside me and I suddenly realized "Oh my God that's me". Different topics would come up and I would think, I did that, and, "I had no idea that I was hurting someone with... "and then I learned that I was suffering from (PTSD) Post Traumatic Stress Disorder. This disorder I found out could be triggered by anything and my reaction to it was probably way out there. Until I recognized the triggers I couldn't stop the behavior. I knew something was wrong and I was trying to learn. I was asking questions for years and no one had any answers. I had blank areas that needed to be filled in but no one could give me the answers. Then at one of the conferences, I attended a session called "Adults Burned as Children".They were talking about a 7 year old little girl who had been burned by a candle. Her clothes caught fire and she was severely burned.

As part of the presentation a film was shown. Within the first 10 seconds seeing this little girl in the film I started to shake and I couldn't control myself. I was now seeing myself and I had to get out of there. Lucky for me that the psychologist who was putting on this seminar recognized what was happening and came to my room and talked with me. There were two other burn survivors with me who helped me through this. I called my sister Susanne in Ontario and cried to her, "Why didn't you tell me, why"? She began crying with me and asking "Tell you what"? "Tell me about how bad it was and the bandages and the pain. Oh the pain, Susanne it hurt so bad." She then told me they weren't allowed to tell me anything. My family were told to let me remember first, and then answer the questions. I was crying and sobbing and in excruciating pain, trying to talk and I couldn't catch my breath or make sense of what I was asking but Susanne knew and she was feeling my pain. Now I remembered everything about that day and now I would get the answers. After attending more of these sessions I also learned that the people around me who saw what happened, were also victims. I had never thought about it that way before. I only thought of myself as the victim. How did it affect them? I was the one who had all this happen to me. But, I was wrong. These other people were mentally affected by what they saw.

After one conference I came home and I looked up the name of the person who had been living with us when I got burned. He had run out in fear and left me and I had not given it another thought. But at the conference they said it was important to make contact and let them know you were doing fine and how were they after all these years. When I reached the fellow I was looking for, he was shocked to hear from me. He thought I was dead, but after convincing him that it was indeed me, we got together in a local coffee shop and talked for a couple of hours. He told me how he never forgot the image of me on fire and that he had felt guilty all his life for not helping me. Through all these years he thought I had died in the fire. He said it had quite an impact on him when raising his own children because like me he was afraid to let his kids near the stove. I thanked him for meeting with me and that I was truly sorry that it took so many years for him to find out the truth but that I hoped he could heal now.

I also contacted both of my ex- husbands and told them how sorry I was for all the commotion I had caused them and for hurting them. That it was me, not them that had done anything wrong. I was so out of control trying to prove to everyone that I was normal like them that I lost touch with the reality of the situation. My second husband told me he knew what was wrong, but that I was not emotionally in the place I am now and would not have listened to him. He was right. I was not in this frame of mind then as I had nothing to show me or no one to tell me. There was no one who had been in my shoes and understood what I was going through with regards to the burns. There was absolutely nothing until now. And now I had become a great student in all things "burns". I flourished and grew and got stronger all the time.

As far as the rape goes, there was nothing I could do and I had to get on with it. Yes, I was paranoid when someone came up behind me but I didn't talk about it. I healed and it was as if it never happened, it was never talked about, and it didn't exist.

It was never far from my mind but when the perpetrator died I felt justice was done and there was nothing more for me to do but live as best I could.

The spousal abuse took me longer to get over because I had become accustomed to being hit for just about everything. I don't think it's completely gone because I still cower sometimes in play with my current partner. He was a huge part of my recovery from the abuse, assuring me that he would never lay a hand on me. He never has. Sometimes when I am in certain situations, I can be intimidated by a person who is bigger in height or weight because it reminds me of him. It takes me time to build up trust .In the normal course of life there is always going to be someone, somewhere who can intimidate you. My father was not a good father. He was not there for his children and I would go as far as to say that we were a burden to him, especially me. One thing for sure is that he was a nasty drunk.

His drinking was mostly on the weekends but it was hell for us. When he was angry at me for whatever reason he would constantly tell me how much I had cost him over the years because of my accident. He didn't have insurance and because of me, he had to do without things he wanted. He told me at one time that I wasn't supposed to live. Incredibly, as I mentioned before, while I was in hospital they made an application to adopt a son. Basically I was being replaced. This hurt a lot and put a strain on my relationship with my brother. It wasn't my brother's fault but it was always in the back of my mind.

My father, a heavy smoker, eventually contracted throat cancer. It was me who took him to his radiation therapies. It was me who was with him when he died. It was me who made the arrangements for his funeral. It was me.

Before he passed he was on palliative care at home and he had us, one at a time, come to his room so he could talk to us. He asked me to forgive him. I asked him for what part. The part that he put us through hell with his running around? The part that he was a nasty drunk? The part where he did nothing to protect his daughter who had been raped? The part where I cost him so much money from my accident? The part where I was put on display? What part did he want forgiveness for? He asked me to forgive all of it. I started crying and told him I understood that he was dying and that he needed this from me but I could not give it to him right now but someday I would forgive him and I would come to his grave and tell him so. I still have not done so. Maybe now that I have put all this in writing, I will be able to shed this anger at him and forgive him. I don't want to be like him and I have set my life as such not to be like him. But as much as I try, I can still see parts of him in me. My kids say I try to control them too much. They may be right and I do listen to them when they tell me this. I have followed in his footsteps with regards to a camping club we have all been involved with. He was president of it for 25 years.

We kids basically grew up there and continued to be there with our own trailers and raised our kids there. Now Mom and Dad are gone and I am President of this club and our kids are now coming in with their own trailers. It's such a blessing to see that this club was started as a family based club and has continued after all these years to still have the same values.

Dad died in March 1994 and Mom died in October 2002. Mom was being taken care of by my other sibling in her home. We realized that Mom could not look after herself and was a danger to herself. When Mom fell ill, and dementia had set in, it became hard on my sibling to look after her alone and I took it upon myself to help her out on weekends. It wasn't much but it gave her a break. I did this for 2 ½ years. I would often sit in the chair when Mom was sleeping and look at her and wonder why I was looking after her when she couldn't look after me.

Having written all of this, has helped me to see more clearly what a sad life my mother had with my father. She loved him so much and he destroyed her. There were some happy times but unfortunately they were few and far between. There were times when I thought I couldn't go on, with all the operations, the bullying and the abuse. In my darkest moment the thought entered my mind that it would be easier to commit suicide. But that thought quickly left me as I knew I was stronger than that. I put a lot of trust in my faith and it was not unusual for me to drop in to my church and just sit there and talk to God. I always felt better when I was ready to leave.

For other burn survivors, we have to learn to love ourselves first and the rest will follow. Talk with other burn survivors, for we are the only ones who know how we suffered, what we have been through and what lies ahead. We have to make our own journey, a new life, in this new skin. It was not what we had foreseen our futures to be but it is our new reality. When we leave the security of the hospital, we have to face this new reality. Seek out your psychiatrist. We leave the hospital stating that, "We are Fine", but we're not. We need to be able to talk with someone because depression can set in very quickly and PTSD can creep up on us before we know or understand it, so we need the psychiatrist to help us through this part of recovery.

For victims of abuse, talk to someone, anyone. I know first-hand that it is easier said, than done. When you are in that situation, you don't see a way out but there always is. You just have to take it, when you have the opportunity. Trust in the justice system for the help you may need to get out of the abuse and away from the abuser.

For victims of rape, the laws have changed today and there is much more awareness around this subject. All I can say is, I didn't get the closure I needed as a teenager and it haunted me for a very long time. Don't be afraid to press charges. Don't let the rapist have that power over you. Remember above all, "It's not your fault".

And so for now this has been my life, one survival moment after another and I hope to continue winning the battle. I have overcome a lot in my past years. I joined the burn support group. I sought psychiatric help. I kept my faith in God. I rejected the idea of suicide. I constantly analyzed the situations I found myself in, trying to find solutions. I studied and applied self-therapy. I got out of my comfort zone many times (i.e. leaving the burn camp and psyching myself up and then going back in).

I didn't blame God for my mishaps. I didn't blame society. I didn't come out hating the world. I even befriended people who had turned away from me at the time of my accident. This is who I am and today I can say, "I am a Survivor".

ABOUT THE AUTHOR

Deborah has had many ups and downs throughout her life but refuses to let life's hurdles keep her down. Born in 1954, Deborah has lived all her life in Nova Scotia.

Deborah is the mother of three children, two daughters and a son, eight grandchildren, step mom to two children and foster Mom to four boys.
Deborah devotes most of her time to burn support through local organizations.

She is President of the Nova Scotia Burn Support Group, Secretary/Treasurer for the Canadian Burn Survivor Community, President of the Avon Boat Club (former boat racing club now a camping club) and a hospital volunteer. She speaks frequently with other burn survivors on a person to person basis and through the Internet on Facebook's Burn Victim Survivor site.

Deborah is an accomplished speaker and is available for presentations at schools, clubs, service organizations, etc.

Dream Hell; Living A Nightmare
Written by: Susanne Blaney | February 8, 2011

Again, the dream
Dream, hell. The nightmare
Does it ever end?
I am now a senior
It's so hard to believe it happened so long ago.
The mind is an amazing entity.
I cannot remember people's names
Or names of places, but
I cannot forget the events of old.
It seems like yesterday rather
Than many, many yesterday's ago.
I'm a child of six or seven
Fingers at my mouth
Shaking. Not from cold but
Absolute fear.
Wondering when will the first blow land.
Or being screamed at and
Being lost and confused as to
"What have I done?"
The hollow feeling in the pit of my belly
When being dismissed with
"Get your ugly face out of my sight".
Lying underneath the covers of the bed
The shaking does not stop.
The feeling of guilt about something I cannot comprehend.
The confusion.
The tears.
The tears of being unloved.
My sense of self pounded into the earth.
You have seen me.
There are many of me out there.

The ones with the uncombed hair
And the wrinkled, unwashed clothes.
Often we're hungry. We smell
Some use drugs or alcohol.
Some steal to get their needs met.
Others prostitute.
Most of us are angry. Many have attitudes,
We don't fit in at school, so we don't go.
It's hard to concentrate when you've been beaten
Mentally and physically,
Oh. It's still happening today.
We are out there.
When you see us don't look at us with scorn.
That's a look we know, even if we don't understand.
Reach out and embrace us.
If you can't do it physically
Because you don't know us
Or due to job restrictions
Embrace us in your heart.
Don't reject us. I need you. We need you.
Share your smile. Say a pleasant word.
We may not respond, but we will remember.
Pray for me. Pray for us.

Shannon Park

1st communion dress

May 24, 1961

Search For New Ideals

"India today is searching for ideals which perhaps only Christianity can provide." Rt Rev Kenneth Annand, Bishop of Amritsar, India, told a missionary rally Tuesday night at the Anglican Diocesan Centre, College Street

The influence of Christianity in India was strong, he said, and many of India's leaders, Christian and non - Christian, read the Bible daily to obtain inspiration and draw strength from it

USE SCRIPTURE

Bishop Annand said it was common for non-Christian leaders to make liberal use of Scriptural texts in their public addresses

Bishop Annand said India today was at a critical and important point in her development and "there are great opportunities which we cannot let pass by"

He said the work of the Church had been recognized and respected by the leaders and the people of India. He cited the great humanitarian work done by Christians during the Partition of India in helping the injured and displaced.

The Canadian Anglican Church was praised highly by Bishop Annand for its work in his diocese — one of India's largest. It covers 144,000 square miles in northwest India in Kashmir and Punjab.

15 CANADIANS

The first bishop of the diocese was a Nova Scotian — the Rt Rev. H. Wilkinson — and at present there are 15 Canadians working in the missions there. Bishop Annand is the first native Indian bishop of the diocese.

Canon H. L. Puxley, president of the University of King's College who spent 14 years in India, introduced Bishop Annand. Mrs. Annand also spoke.

Rt. Rev. Reginald J. Pierce, Bishop of Athabaska in Canada addressed the rally on the work being done in Canada's north by the Anglican Church In Nova Scotia for the Dio

Girl Burned, Boy Hurt In Separate Accidents

Seven-year-old Deborah Alice Blaney of Shannon Park is still in critical condition at the Children's Hospital this morning following an accident in her home yesterday noon.

She was severely burned on the chest and legs when her clothes caught on fire after she had leaned over the stove. Her mother, Mrs. Eric Blaney, received minor burns when she attempted to stamp out the fire and was treated at the Victoria General Hospital and released.

The father and husband, Chief Petty Officer Eric Blaney, at the time of the accident, was on board HMCS Haida which was scheduled to arrive in port at 11 a.m. this morning.

Donald Scott, eight-year-old son of Mr. and Mrs. Ross Scott of Waverley Road, Bedford, is in satisfactory condition in the Victoria General Hospital this morning following a highway accident.

He received a fractured skull when he was involved in collision with a truck, noon Tuesday.

Head Women's Press Club

Mrs. W. E. Colpitts (Joan Marshall) was elected president of the Nova Scotia branch of the Canadian Women's Press Club in Halifax at last night's annual meeting.

Other officers: vice-president, Miss Margaret Healey; secretary-treasurer, Mrs. Vincent Coade; corresponding secretary, Miss Mary Casey; program chairman, Miss Marion Moore; membership chairman, Miss

MISSIONARY AIDED —
Local Council of the Anglican Young People's Association, held its annual banquet in the hall of St. John's Church, Tuesday night, when Father Jonathan Onyemelukwe of Nigeria was presented with a cheque by president Miss Marion Conrad, Miss Helen Dauphinee, publicity convener, books on. (Wamboldt).

PORTABLES POPULAR
NEW YORK (UPI) — Of the 20.4 million radio sets sold in the U.S. at retail in 1960, more than 8 million were portables, the Radio Advertising Bureau, Inc. reports.

Members of the Halifax Y's Men's Club are asked to attend the funeral of the late Y's Bob Cornfine at Cruikshanks Funeral Home, Robie St., Thursday, May 25, at 10.30 a.m.

Signed
Y's John Fraser,
Secretary.

TO LET
2 Office suites approximately 800 sq. ft. each. Centrally located in main business section of Kentville directly across from Post Office Occupancy — June & July. Can be made suitable for almost any type of business. Apply to George Wade—Kentville, Nova Scotia.

Call PRYOR CONSTRUCTION LTD.
Let an expert do it! Repairs and Renovations for Office, Home and Plant. Small jobs. Dept. Call for estimate.
BLAND ST, • Tel. 423-8341

Newspaper article, May 24, 1961

Debbie at 14 years old

1st husband

2nd wedding

3rd marriage

Printed in Canada